UNVEILING
Reality

UNVEILING
Reality

THE AWAKENING OF
CORE-SPLITTING HONESTY

JOHN DE RUITER

THE COLLEGE OF
INTEGRATED PHILOSOPHY

UNVEILING REALITY Copyright ©2019 College of Integrated Philosophy.
First published as a paperback March 2000.
Second printing - February 2001.
Revised Second Edition - April 2019.
All rights reserved.
Printed in Canada.

No portion of this book may be used or reproduced in any manner whatsoever without written permission, except in the case of brief quotations embodied in critical articles or reviews. For information address College of Integrated Philosophy, 10930-177 Street Edmonton, AB, Canada T5S 2X7

ISBN 9781790122998
College of Integrated Philosophy Publishing
10930-177 Street Edmonton, AB, Canada T5S 2X7

Contents

FOREWORD VII

INTRODUCTION IX

ON A SPIRITUAL PATH 1

SPIRITUALITY 21

INNERMOST – OUTERMOST 47

THE TINY LITTLE BIT 75

ENLIGHTENMENT THROUGH ENDARKENMENT 93

TENDER HONESTY IS A CURE-ALL 109

THAT STILL SMALL VOICE 139

Foreword

This book was originally printed in the year 2000, compiled from live dialogues between John and individuals from around the world seeking true meaning in their lives. When in dialogue with John, the speaker often enters a field beyond time, space, and language, in which the deeper senses awaken, and we meet truth face to face.

We wake up from the sweetest dream, but the memory fades; we sense something greater and lovelier than this routine life, but forget again. John guides us into the meaning, and we are able to remain there, so that we can truly live our realization. We become aware of what is deeper, leading us into openness and softness of heart, and a core-splitting honesty that lives simply for what it knows to be true.

John's teaching has evolved over the years but the heart of it remains unchanged as these classic dialogues illustrate. John unveils the truth that is already within us, yet gently states what is worth living for. This book marks a fundamental period in John's life in which honesty and knowing are defined as the cornerstone of his teaching. Long out of print, an updated edition of Unveiling Reality is a highly anticipated jewel.

As you read, remember that the words here were spoken between real people, from one open heart to another. The heart is their origin and their resting place. An open and soft heart is enough to fulfill a whole life-time. Through it, endless meaning opens up. John's meetings awaken us to the world within, and as magnificent as that is, it begins simply with a "yes" to the tiny little bit you know is true.

Introduction

We humans have such an awesome capacity. We have a full spectrum of consciousness. Through the vehicles of the mind, body, emotion, will and intuition, we can experience endlessly expansive or endlessly intricate dimensions of inward and outward movement of being. Within that, as we can later come to know, we have the capacity to share in profound depths of oneness with the universe.

And what we also have is power – the ultimate kind of power, the greatest power in the entire universe: we have the power to choose to be anything we prefer, real or illusory, unlike the rest of existence which can only be itself.

As beings, we recognize what moves us and what we love most within those rich and diverse experiences of humanness. We clearly know the flow of goodness beneath the sensory wrappings, and we love it. It is the human heart – consciousness, finding itself in love with the truth from which it originates, the truth that touches it and nourishes it in so many different ways within.

Those formless touches of being, which come wrapped in sensory experience, quieten and gentle our hearts and nourish us purely. They are beautiful and they are true. But instead of residing in that same true way of being, allowing those touches to move through us as easily as they moved into us, we find their beauty for ourselves. We identify with the vehicles of form through which those touches of being came, and we begin to create an identity. We isolate what brings us joy and peace, and we begin to desire that; we begin to require that. We as consciousness actually have the capacity to hold onto those experiences, claim personal ownership of them, grasp anything we find pleasing and force away whatever is not. We have the power to abandon a complete and true way of being for an inherently deficient path of self-gratification.

And that is the beginning of our own distortion as consciousness. The more space we give for an illusory identity of want and need, the less room there will be for what is real. Soon, we cannot even identify what reality is. And then we begin to seek.

This mistaken identity of being will lead us to falsely search for a seemingly elusive reality: the truth that we know exists, but somehow can no longer find. It is we as consciousness, erroneously identifying ourselves as the vehicles of expression, instead of recognizing and surrendering to the reality of pure consciousness, love, truth itself, which expresses itself through them.

In that self-oriented way of being, everything we touch and everything we do becomes tainted. If what we are living for is to take the nourishment and beauty of truth or love for the satisfaction of the senses – to feel good, to be at peace, to have something we can claim as our own – then we find ourselves continuously seeking and never truly finding. We have become a consciousness residing in a way of insistent desire, instead of in a true way of being, like the truth itself that we have tasted and now hunger to regain.

Ironically, the very truth we are in love with most has always shown us how to be. What we are really in love with most is the true intimacy of inner rest, softness and tenderness. We are truly in love with the only way of being that satisfies and nurtures us completely. But as consciousness, we create a personal love based on self-oriented longing. We become a consciousness that replaces intimacy of true being with the personalness of dishonest striving. We become restless and we harden inside in our effort to hold and control. We exchange the gentle and tender manner of a real way of being, for one of inner labour and insistence. We lose the goodness we know is true, and we gain a goodness we think and feel is true, based on indulgence in personal wishes and dreams.

We lose our connection with reality; we lose our way. We lose the integrity of surrendering to the only reality, because we have created a private, inherently empty reality instead.

As a young man of seventeen, I was unexpectedly gifted with a knowing and an experience of oneness with the source: an intimate universe on the inside and at the same time an equally intimate universe on the outside. I was conscious and clear between the two, yet I was being in the oneness of both at the same time. My awareness of reality expanded in ways that I could never have imagined. I experienced joy, love and deep, inner rest, and I became dearly re-connected to a true way of being, that at the time, I could not comprehend with my mind.

That true way of being slowly dissipated and after one year, everything vanished as quickly as it had come. I found myself feeling profoundly empty and incomplete. I thought that life could only be meaningless and superficial without the intimacy and the nectar of experiencing oneness with the source, reality, truth, and without the contentment of the nourishing way of being I had come to reside in. Yet in the midst of what seemed like incredible loss, I had a tiny, little knowing: I still knew the true way of gentleness and rest that I had so warmly been re-acquainted with throughout that year, though I could not understand nor experience it.

Instead of simply residing in that way of being I knew was true, at any personal cost to my emotions and mind, I initially attempted to regain the sensations of truth. When I allowed my own honesty to become finer, I realized it was not experience itself that mattered, just truth. But I thought I had lost my way. I began to strive and search intensely through many different means, relentlessly pursuing anything I believed might show me the way back. And as consciousness, that took me deeper and deeper within myself. I allowed honesty to look at each doctrine, each teacher and each technique I encountered, only to discover that they were all less than absolutely true. I became completely devastated. Each time I discovered yet another untruth, I let myself drop even deeper within. As consciousness, I was at the bottom of my own well, a well I had carved out through letting myself be continuously cracked open, deeper and deeper – and there was no water.

At last, through simplicity of heart, through pure and absolute honesty, I just simply let go. I surrendered, unconditionally to just simply being at the bottom of that well of darkness and never again trying to get out, warmly never again hoping for water. And it was at that moment that I became re-immersed in the benevolent reality of pure being. I became filled with the same absolutely immaculate reality of truth I had known before, only this time to the depths that I had inwardly allowed myself to be hollowed out. I now knew that I not only loved truth more than my own personal life, but that truth could only be truly known through sheer honesty and surrender in openness and softness to what that honesty reveals. Truth is loving reality with an open hand, instead of pursuing reality with the clenched hand of personal necessity and demand.

There was a continuum of awakenings that followed over the years. I remained in constant honesty and surrender to what I knew was true, allowing my own self-created constructs and attachments of mind and emotion to die. And as that took place, my ability to function as integrated consciousness – to function as a being of what I am in love with most – began to live. More and more deeply I realized that I would only serve truth; I would live in surrender to what I know, at any personal cost. I am no longer my own; I belong to truth. I have no interest in power or personal identity, just a love of true being, upheld by an absolute inner honesty of heart.

It is so easy for everyone to just simply rest as consciousness in that same true way of being. All it requires is untainted surrender to what you honestly know is true, and all it will cost is your personal wants and needs. All it will cost is just your personal dream, your illusion. Then, as you continue to let in truth to the point where it has replaced everything in you that is untrue, then you come into true form. You come to know your real self, and you come to realize and live the reality you were in when you were very, very young. You begin to grow as a real human being, a beloved servant of truth, instead of a slave of your own illusion.

Truth is so easy; it is so consummately nourishing and complete. It is everything we have always been looking for, and yet it has always been here, right here within our own hearts, within us as consciousness. Truth is consciousness, but our own distortions conceal it. Truth has always been so close, so accessible, it only waits for our open door. And the greatest power we have as human beings is choice. We can choose to create our own gates of illusion and create everything they will enclose, or we can open the door and simply let reality in; just let its purity and profound goodness completely consume us. It is all up to us. But the moment we open that door – even just a crack – if we let ourselves be honest inside, then what we will find is totally irresistible.

John de Ruiter
February, 2000

Waking up is not necessarily pleasant.
You get to see
why all this time
you chose to sleep.

When you wake up,
the first thing you will see is
reality does not exist for you,
you exist for it.
Shocking as it is,
when you let it in,
there is rest.

You do not have to labour anymore
to hold together a reality
that does not exist,
forcing something to be real
that is not real.

You and this life you have been living
are not real.

In letting it in,
even through the shock, pain, shattering,
there is rest.

Reality is when
all you want to know is
what is true,
just so that you can
let it in
and be true.

Reality is not a safe place for you —
the you that you have created.
It is the only place where
you would die,
where there is no room for
your hopes, your dreams.

Once you have let it in,
once you begin to re-awaken,
to let reality wake you up,
nothing can get it out.
That is the beginning of your end.
Waking up can be much more painful
than the agony of your dream,
but waking up is real.

And there will be integration:
a merging of reality and you.
You and reality will become one
in a world that does not
accept nor want one,
but two.

You will become a beloved servant
instead of a controlling master.

The following seven chapters are the revised transcripts compiled from live meetings with John de Ruiter and his audience, held in Edmonton and Vancouver, Canada; London and Bristol, UK; and Boulder, U.S.A in 1998 & 1999.

The text of this book is comprised of John's teachings, with all audience questions appearing in italics for clarity.

CHAPTER 1

On a Spiritual Path

All there is
that counts for anything at all
is what honesty knows is true,
and it lives for that
and it dies for that;
it is everything for that.
It is just a one way flow –
everything that you are
for what you know is true.

You finally get to give up all of your rights:
your right to love, happiness, pain relief, peace,
your right of way.
And all that remains
that has any right of way,
ever again, is
the tiniest little bit
that you know is true.

There is nothing easier.
That is what this life is for.
That is what the surface bodies are for:
living vehicles to express truth,
not what we want or need.
When we are quieted and gentled inside,
we actually know.

I. ON A SPIRITUAL PATH

Questioner: I have a question about exertion and discipline. In some traditions exertion is part of one's path of surrender. In the Buddha's path, discipline is very important and exertive prostration is part of the exertion. Does exertion have a place here in your teachings?

John: So it is using a structure to find the part of you that is formless, that has no structure?

Well, it's also using the body in a certain disciplined way.

Being in the body, functioning in form, that is good. But if one is engaging the mind and the will with the body to attain reality within consciousness or the heart, that will not work. That is using focus of the mind and will, together with the vehicle of physical form, as tools to isolate and acquire something formless. The will and the mind cannot attain truth, reality, being. They cannot be used to acquire the formless reality of truth or being, within the heart. Nothing in form: not one or any combination of the surface vehicles of expression such as the mind, emotions, body, will and intuition, or any structure, discipline or exertion, can be used as a tool in attaining the formless reality of a true way of being within the heart.

No amount of doing through any of the surface vehicles can achieve this. Once you have surrendered all outer doing to an inner way of being that is true, then that true way of being which originates in the heart, in the innermost of consciousness, can really be expressed in form through the surface vehicles. But this is a one way flow from the innermost outward. It cannot be achieved from the outside in. You cannot do to be.

I get that on one level, but I don't get it on a deep level.

On a deep level, why would you ever do to be, when you could just be? If you could attain it without the discipline, without the focus, without the tools of doing year after year after year, would you still do to be?

I wouldn't want to say I spent all those years doing A, B, C and found out that it was all unnecessary. I am referring to the discipline, meditation, prostration, gurus and certain kinds of learning. I just can't discount it all, just like that.

So you are going to continue to do it all?

No, I was just referring to what I have done in the past. And then to hear that, for instance, books really don't help and learning doesn't help, I can't warmly embrace it.

Because you have already put an investment into it?

That's certainly part of it.

But if you are about to put tremendous investment into that, and it is possible that you do not have to do any of that, would it bother you?

You mean if I was just starting out on the spiritual path? That's hard to say. I have been so entrenched, the discipline part is really part of my life. That's what I mean by entrenched.

What has that entrenchment done for you?

It kept me on the spiritual path.

What has that spiritual path done for you?

Well, I am here.

I. ON A SPIRITUAL PATH

Before now, what has it done for you? All those years, what has the spiritual path done for you?

I was able to recognize my being.

And what is it like?

I know that there is a deeper part of me than just the mundane aspects of life.

But even before you embarked on a path, the moment you were quiet inside, you knew the same thing – there is a much deeper part of you than the life you are acquainted with on the surface.

Yes, I think I knew that, but I still wanted to connect more or be in that deeper part more.

When people are on a path, particularly if they are serious about it, they do open up to greater depths within consciousness, and they do soften. And there is also something else that happens. There is this very fine, intricate, sophisticated internal structure that forms. A structure concerning them getting more: more sophisticated, more knowledge, knowing how to move, knowing how to be, knowing how to flow. And there is a something in it for them. It is not just free. It matters that they are like that. It matters that they are seen like that. And anyone who is not like that is seen as less.

So there is a certain spiritual superiority? I have been like that.

That will always happen in being on a path. If you are on a path, you are not on a path for what is true, you are on a path for yourself. So anything that happens on that path is acquired by you. That path is taken so that the coarse *somebody* can turn into a sophisticated, spiritually refined *somebody*.

If you are interested in truth, then there will not be a path at all. If truth is all you really want, just so that you can give yourself to it, then there is an immediate surrender within: a total surrender of all that you are doing and all that you have acquired for yourself in being a somebody, and there is a simple resting in consciousness within. That rest from striving and doing for self-created agendas is you as consciousness finally residing in a way of being that is true. It is you as consciousness returning home.

You will recognize and you will know the truth of that way of being the moment you let yourself be in it. That openness and softness of consciousness within is the true way of being that everyone actually knows about. It requires honesty of consciousness to see it. And it requires a love of true seeing to let yourself surrender to it. Then you become less of a somebody. Then there is a losing of everything that in reality is already dead inside.

Individuals who go on a path are not on a path to lose something, to give something up to what they know is true. They are on a path to get. Being on a path, they end up acquiring. Instead of being on a path, there can be a complete surrender to what they as consciousness actually know is true, regardless of how tiny that may seem to be.

You could surrender everything that you are, surrender your entire existence just because that is true, not because it does something for you. With that kind of surrender, whatever kind of somebody you are, all is given up. You do not get anything out of it. It is what you know is true that actually gets you. When there is the use of techniques, exertion, discipline and focus, it is always done for oneself.

And to develop compassion.

For whom? Why would you try to develop compassion?

To help other people, to connect with others, to be loving toward others, because it is an aspiration. I don't see compassion as being totally self-centred. I see it as going out, like there is the stream, then becoming the ocean of compassion. It's not just focused on myself.

Then what is it focused on?

It's focused on others out of love.

As soon you are interested in loving people, you become a somebody. You become much more of a sophisticated somebody: a very loving somebody, a very kind somebody, a compassionate and gentle somebody. And people easily aspire to that, because when they are being loving and kind and compassionate and gentle that really feels good. But it is not good, because it is done for themselves. It is not really done for others.

What is happening is more like using someone to have something to love, because if you have nothing to love then you have nothing inside. Then you are empty. So then the individuals who are being loved are being used. And that love is not an unconditional love.

What if the person you were loving were to make it their life's purpose to hurt you and destroy you and tear you down, and never stop until they die? Would you hesitate in loving that person? All you would have to do is just simply not love that person and everything would be fine. Would you hesitate? Would you skip that person and go to a different one?

If a person is being loving and that love is real, then it would not matter how deeply you went inside of that person as consciousness. You would never find a line. There would be no button to be pushed. You could push and abuse and take advantage. You could do absolutely anything as deeply as you could possibly reach inside of that person to hurt them. The deeper you reached, the greater the depth of love there would be, and there would be no faltering, no failing.

But if someone is using his or her will and efforting to be loving, all you have to do is touch that person's will, and that love will turn around. It will not look so nice anymore. It will turn into frustration, anger, hatred. We use people as something to love, and when they dislike it or do not appreciate what it is that we are using them for, we get upset. If they are not cooperating with our loving them, we become unhappy. But if they are really cooperative, then we feel happy because we think and feel we are really experiencing being loving. And deep inside we remain empty.

When the loving we have been doing has not touched us deep within, has not addressed what we know is true deep within us as consciousness, then any happiness we have acquired is equally shallow, equally dissatisfying. It does not fulfill, because it does not originate from our innermost being. That kind of love is not powerful, not real, because it is not a natural flow of expression originating from an innermost way of being that is absolutely and purely true. So it keeps us perpetually needing to love, and perpetually hungering for more of an incomplete kind of love that, on the inside, we actually know we have no need of at all.

The only way that you can be trusted with love that is truly powerful, love that is real, is: could you first be unconditionally and warmly okay with losing your capacity to love and also losing your capacity to be loved? If that were to be taken away, stripped away and gone for good, such that you would never get it back, could you be as warmly okay in being that loveless, unlovable person, okay that it would never need to change? That is love.

Inasmuch as we are addicted to wanting love, then any love we are giving is something we are putting together, because we cannot live without it. We cannot accept ourselves if we do not have that, if we are not like that. So then our loving of people is just a garment we wear. And we will put on the best garment. Being on a path is always looking for more. Everything we find, we accumulate, and then we become more. We become a *somebody* who really has *something*.

When you are living in what you know is true, living in a way of being that originates from your innermost of consciousness, you never try to acquire more. What happens is you become warmly content with less and less and less. Within you as consciousness, you are never looking for more. You are perpetually in love with less. And then as a being, as consciousness, as a heart, the less you become, the finer your way of being becomes.

When your way of being is no longer full of will, mind and emotion and there is no more agenda, then all that remains is just an openness and a space for the formless reality of truth or being, within you as consciousness, to express itself in any way it does. The more you love to simply give everything away to that way of being, the more that way of being will occupy your space. There will be no path, because you are giving your wants and your needs away. There will simply be a true way of being: an openness and a softness and a surrender to what you honestly know is true. Regardless of what that brings or does not bring, you would be deeply satisfied. There could be no path. You would be living without a path, simply, in a way of being that is true.

There are no nobodies who have nothing, and are content with less, who are on a path. Being on a path is being on a path away from what we know is true. It is being on a path to more: more of what we want, more of what we prefer, more of what we think we need. So then we work hard and read books, study, take courses and involve ourselves in disciplines that, inside, we are not really loyal to. If you could get what you wanted without ever meditating, you would never meditate again.

Well, there is a certain thing that develops. With meditation you become the watcher. It's more self-focused in a sense.

The watcher is much more of a sophisticated, practised somebody. The watcher will not surrender to what it actually knows is true, because then it will disappear inside of what it knows is true, and then there will be no more watcher. The watcher keeps itself safe.

How does one give up the watcher?

By surrendering to what one honestly knows is true. When you as consciousness let honesty in, then immediately you begin to see everything – everything that you are holding onto, everything you are wanting. The moment you see what it is that you want, there will be a knowing that you do not need that. There will be an inner surrender to letting it go. One of the things you will be surrendering is being the watcher.

What remains is you merging with what you know is true. You become that. And the you that you are accustomed to, including the watcher, will be gone. The you that you are used to will become extinct. It will all be over. Self-ownership will be gone. Living for yourself will be gone. Living for happiness, living for peace and love and joy will be gone. You will be living for what you know is true, just because that is what is true, not because of any benefit to you. And now it will no longer make any difference whether there is suffering because of loving what you know is true and surrendering to it, or whether there is gain.

Then, if perceived happiness in one avenue and perceived unhappiness in another were to present themselves to you, and you could go one way or the other, you would never choose the one over the other. As soon as a choice could be made between the two, all you would do within is open and soften and rest in what you know to be true and let that knowing carry you either way. There would be no preference. You would only be interested in which one is most true.

If both were true – but there was a knowing that it was just a little bit more true to go in the direction of perceived unhappiness for the rest of your life, that everything would go badly instead of easily on a road of happiness – then would you, without hesitation, surrender to what you know is true? If you were to go down the road of perceived happiness, but year after year after year there would be that odd little touch that it was a tiny bit more true to go down the road of unhappiness, then, if you really wanted what is true, you would go back. You would go down the road of perceived unhappiness. If you were to remain on the road of happiness, you would always be going down that road rationalizing and justifying why you are on a path. That path would be all about you. If it were really about what you know is true, then without hesitation you would turn around. You would be in love with going down that path of perceived unhappiness just because of your knowing of truth.

When you do what is right, what you perceive is right but, for you, then all that happens is you become self-righteous. Everything that you change or alter inside, when you do it for you, just makes the self-righteousness become even finer and more cunning, more sophisticated. It will even look better.

But as soon as you realize that, then you can give it all up, let it all go. Not for you, but for the little bit that you honestly know is true. There is a knowing you have that the small amount you do know is really true. It is worth more than all of you put together; it is worth more than your life; it is worth more than your feelings and your thoughts. And the moment you allow yourself to realize that knowing, then you can live for that.

Then you are no longer on a path. Then you are free-falling inside of the least amount that you actually know is true. Then there is no more hesitation in you as consciousness; there is no looking back. All you are is warmly and supremely in love with anything that you really know is true. And it is never done for the sake of you.

When there is that kind of surrender, then, when love happens, you will not be in it. When there is a love toward someone, it will be a kind of love that is not conditioned by your realization that when you love, it feels good. It will not be conditioned by your realization that when you love someone, he or she will make way for you; that your capacity to get what you want from that person really increases.

When the surrender is done for the sake of you, there is the recognition inside that when you love, that is the most powerful way of controlling. It is realized very quickly. There is a genius at work that puts it all together. Even little children, the moment they realize this, begin to do it. When we get older we learn how to hide it. We learn how to be really, really smooth. We are expert at disguise. We cannot afford anyone seeing what we are doing, because then we would be exposed. Instead of being this loving, nice, kind, gentle, giving, compassionate person, we would be exposed as a scoundrel, and then we would no longer be trusted. We could not bear not being trusted, and we could not bear being seen that way.

So as children we have this inner knowing in truth, and then it gets manipulated and covered up?

Our inner knowing interferes with what we want. As soon as something interferes with what we want, we cover it. If what we are wanting is to surrender to what we know is true, just because that is of more value than our life or anything else that we could ever want, then instead of covering up what we know is true there would be such a fine sensitivity. We would surrender to just the tiniest amount of what we should find that we know is true, even if it were to cost us our whole life, because we love truth more than our life. So there would be no hesitation. Then truth would be uncovered, instead of covered up.

Being on a path is looking for the kind of truth that really suits and serves what we want. It is not looking for the kind of truth that serves what we know is true. It only serves what we want. So someone on a path is less safe to be with than some rough, coarse, straightforward "all I want is what I want" kind of person. That individual is just being as is. Nothing is covered. Everything is simple and straightforward.

With someone on a path, everything is covered. Only how that person chooses to be seen is out front. But behind all of that is a learned, skilled seeing and looking. All that person lives for is just to get exactly what he or she wants, and no one is allowed to see that this is what that person is really doing. Someone on a spiritual path is less safe to be with. That person is experienced and skilled at taking advantage of him or herself, of others, and of truth. Someone on a path cannot be trusted with love or truth.

Well, I think one would have to be fearless to go into free fall.

Just honest. It is only honesty of consciousness that can ever be fearless. The only time there is fear is when consciousness is being dishonest. When consciousness is being dishonest, then it is hiding from something that it knows is true. It is creating something else that it knows is not true. It is hiding inside of that and dressing itself inside of that illusion. And now there is fear, because there is this knowing deeper down that something threatens what that person, as consciousness, is living in.

That kind of consciousness or heart believes: "If I don't protect it, then I begin to relax. As soon as I begin to really relax and begin to be okay inside, then I begin to see what it is that I know is true. And I see that what I am in is an illusion. I will end up surrendering the illusion and I will surrender to what I know is true, and then look what I have lost!" When there is fear, that fear is only cloaking something that we are hanging onto that is not ours. And we do not want to see that.

When there is honesty, we begin to see clearly. We begin to see what is inside, what we are hanging onto, what we are cloaking. And then there is an opening, there is a softening, there is a letting-go. And when that happens, fear is displaced with a love of truth – a love of what comes from our innermost. And if that is what we are most in love with, then free falling into what we are in love with is easy. There is no fear, there is no dread of that, because we are only merging with what we are in love with most.

Merging with reality is simply being in love with what we honestly know is true. We even know that it is good, that it is worth everything, that it is worth more than we are. In reality, there is nothing there that could ever touch fear. So it is only in the true, full, complete, absolute kind of honesty that we will let ourselves really see, just so that we can see what is true and give into it. With that kind of honesty, there is never fear. We do not have to be courageous, and we do not have to be strong – just honest.

As long as we are living in fear, as long as fear is there, that totally exposes us. As long as there is fear, that means consciousness is not being honest with something that it knows is true. Fear is just consciousness willingly being dishonest.

Our whole society is dishonest and based on fear.

Totally. We all know it. People look at everyone else and can expose them all, but not themselves. Rarely do people allow themselves to really see and in that seeing, reveal themselves. The fear of real seeing, the fear of exposing what they are hanging onto inside, keeps people from unveiling the reality that they actually know is true. That leads them to an unnatural and unwarranted exertion of power to protect their inner illusion. And that is violence. All of it is just a distortion of consciousness rooted in dishonesty. People think: "I can see what's wrong in you, and I know that it's not right. I don't want to change what's not right in me, because that will cost me something. But I will try to change what's wrong in you." So then they have a dishonest mission, a fear-based self-righteous mission that is unclean, unnatural.

Anyone with an issue has a self-righteous vehemence. That person is on a self-oriented path away from what he or she knows is true. The issue is there to help that person stay very focused inside, so busy that there does not have to be a seeing and a surrender to what he or she knows is true. That person gets to work on something self-oriented instead.

Anyone with an issue manifests violence. All you have to do is cross that issue and there will be an aggression that comes back. There will be a coarseness, there will be a cutting, even if the issue is that we all need to love one another. If, for example, people were to come along and say to the loving person whose issue it is that we all need to love one another, that they instead choose only to live for themselves, that they do not care about anyone else and that if they could, they would use the loving person to get what they want, then you would see what would happen inside of that loving person. The loving person would not be so loving. There would be a judgment. And there would be an edge, a condemnation. If he or she had the power, that loving person would force a change. That loving person would make those people just the way he or she thinks they should be, based on his or her own personal issues.

People with issues cannot be trusted with power. People with issues are wanting something for themselves. If they had power, people with issues would use that power to force a change, to stop anything that is interfering with their personal agenda. People use power to force so they end up with disagreements, reactions, edges. And that is war. Even if people are rallying for peace, that is war.

People who want to be loved unconditionally by the universe are dangerous. If they had the power, they would take that love from the universe. They would tell the universe: "I am ready for all the unconditional love" and if the universe were to not give that love, they would use their power to encourage it a bit. That is being on a path. Only those who need to have an issue with something would ever be on a path. And those who are on a path are violent, because there is something they will illegitimately strive to acquire, only for themselves and for their personal issues. If they had the power to acquire that, they would use it.

Someone who is in a way of being that is true will have no issue with anything. There will be no issue with peace. There will be no issue with inner peace. There will be no wanting. There will not be issues of: "All I need is just a little bit of peace," or "I want to be more loving" or "I ought to be loved unconditionally by the universe." There will be no such issues at all.

Only individuals who, on the inside, have want and need of nothing, can be trusted with anything because they would never use what they received for a want or for a need. If they were to receive power, love, goodness, kindness, or enlightenment, if they were to receive anything at all inside, they would not even touch it for themselves. They would never use it for a feel-good. They would never use it to be able to manifest something for themselves. They would simply remain in what they knew to be true, and none of it would be for them.

But they would be full of something of infinitely greater value than themselves. And they would never take that valuable something and dress themselves with it. They would simply be a safe-keeper. They would devote the everything that they are to just holding it there, because it was given to them in trust. They would never touch it, never use it; they would live being in love with what is inside of them in trust.

A person who, on the inside, truly has want and need of nothing, would not use anything received in trust unless something within what he or she knew to be true – a knowing, a clarity – moved that person to respond in a particular way of goodness, kindness, power or love. Then everything of that person would touch what was being made manifest within them, and embrace it, and utilize it in being true. And in all of the touching, embracing and flowing, that person would still take nothing for him or herself. That is a lover of truth. That is the only kind of person who could ever be trusted, the only kind of person who could truly, unconditionally love. That is the only kind of person who could be unconditionally loved, and not take it for him or herself; they would not want it.

So the only true way is not to be loving nor to seek peace; it is not looking, it is not searching. The only true way is letting honesty open up and at last, letting ourselves see what it is that we know is true. It is giving up everything that we are, just to please and serve and exist for the tiniest little bit that we know is true and of real value. That is truly being loving.

When we surrender ourselves to that, then we never take anything for ourselves. We perpetually give up everything that we are and give it all away, just so that little bit can live out its own expression. It gets to have our space, just to be in and express itself. And if living that way were to take us into perpetual unhappiness and suffering and pain until the day we died, it would be our most dear honour, that this is all it costs, for us to serve what we know is of infinite value. As consciousness, we *get to* give into what we truly love, what we honestly know, at any cost. This is the fulfillment of true happiness.

And what happens when we die? What happens to consciousness?

When we physically die, consciousness will be awakened to reality. You will be awakened to everything that you have been living inside of all your life in terms of wanting, needing, grabbing or feeling *I must have*. When you die, you will be this consciousness that knows it has learned to be violent, but all the things that you have been holding and wanting and needing will be gone. The illusion will be over. You will be intimately pierced with tender pain as you fully realize every moment that you have lied to yourself with the effort of self-protection, every moment that you have turned away from the sweetest touches of being that were wooing you back to your first love – the love of being and the love of what is true.

All that will remain is what has always been there in your innermost that you have been denying and pushing down, abusing, covering and stepping on. It is the only thing that ever existed that really threatened you. It is the only thing you feared and dreaded because you knew that if you let it in, you would lose everything you wanted. You would give up everything you thought you needed. Then you would have become unconditionally and warmly content with less and less and less and less. Those who are on a path, when they die, are in for a shock. Their consciousness is in for a shock.

If you die now then for the rest of your life truth gets to live in you. So you can die to everything that you are wanting and needing and demanding, everything that you have an issue with. You get to let every issue die inside of you. You get to let them all go. And the only life that you will be left living is one that is merging with what you honestly know is true. Then, when you physically die, there will not be a painful shift in consciousness with all of the ensuing shock.

There is something very tricky here about wanting. It seems to get more and more subtle when we start to talk about preparing ourselves to die in the right way. It's similar to the ancient Egyptian perspective on dying.

It is not preparing yourself to die. The wanting and the needing can end at this moment, and you can simply let them die now instead of prolonging it, pushing it forward: "I'll let go tomorrow, I'll let something get inside of me today that I know is not true – I'll let it die tomorrow, later. Right now I want to live my way, for what I want, even if I know it's not true." The ancient Egyptians, in preparing to die for tomorrow, were doing essentially the same thing. It was done for themselves, not because of what they knew was true.

With true dying within consciousness, there is no more wanting, only total honesty of consciousness and total surrender – that's it! No path, no trying, no effort, no tomorrow. Just all of that honesty and surrender now. There is nothing else. Anything else is of a violent denial.

Isn't it a kind of violence to push down your own violence?

It is, because then you have an issue with being violent. Now you are a danger to your true self because you are making being hard on yourself another issue. Striving to push down your violence is just another path, another doing for a self-serving purpose. Every path, structure, labour, technique and discipline used to attain something that serves you is just another avoidance of reality. It is only self-oriented wanting and needing; it is inner dishonesty of consciousness, manifesting in form. It is an outward expression of an inward lack of stillness and rest – a manifestation of an untrue way of being.

It is the same with religion. If you have an issue with needing to be religious, then you are wanting and needing and striving and labouring for yourself. You are trying to achieve something that on the inside, if you just let yourself be completely honest, you actually know you have no need of at all. Using God and using truth to get something for you, is just another form of dishonesty. It is just an avoidance of resting in a true way of being, resting in the truth. It is striving for a truth or striving for your own truth, instead.

A way of being that is true, just simply and immediately and absolutely drops into what it presently knows is true, and lives for that just because that is of value and true.

And that doesn't count for anything because you're not even thinking about it?

Nothing in your life counts for anything. All there is that counts for anything at all is what honesty knows is true. And it lives for that and it dies for that. It is everything for that. It is just a one way flow; everything that you are, for what you know is true. You finally get to give up all your rights: your right to love, your right to happiness, your right to pain relief, your right to peace. You finally get to give up your right of way. And all that remains, that has any right of way ever again, is the tiniest little bit that you know is true. It gets to have right of way. You are in love with knowing that it has the right of way, anywhere inside of you, anywhere in your life; that it could touch anything in you, do anything in you. And all you would ever do is be in love with responding.

It's not nearly as hard as I thought.

There is nothing easier. This is easier than thinking. It is simply residing in a way of being that you know is true. It is home. It is easier than the *you* you have come to identify with, going into your will and making even a touch of effort in any direction. It is easier than that, because then consciousness has to go into the will and do something that it honestly knows it does not need to do. Instead, the will can remain surrendered for true innermost consciousness to go inside of and express itself. The mind, the emotions, the will, the intuition and the body can all remain surrendered as vehicles of expression for true innermost consciousness to flow through. Then true innermost consciousness finally gets to express what it knows is true to express.

That is true expression: a flow of what you live and die to give yourself to, a flow of what you know is true. It is truth or innermost consciousness moving all the way through the real you, through to the outermost of consciousness into the will, the emotions, the mind, the body and the intuition, expressing everything that is so true. And expressing it in a way that is true.

That is what this life is for. That is what the surface bodies are for. Surface bodies begin to die when they are being used to express what you want, and what you need. But in reality the surface bodies get to really, really live as vehicles to express truth. When you are quieted and gentled inside, then you actually know.

CHAPTER 2

Spirituality

Doing "spiritual work" is
fundamental
non-acceptance
of things as they presently are.

There is nothing to change
inside of you;
there is nothing to do,
nothing that you
actually have need of.

Anything that you perceive you
want or need,
you do not.

Mixing spirituality
with anything,
is mixing internal effort
with everything.

That makes everything worse.
That distracts you
from honesty,
from surrender.

Spiritual work is a distraction
into some form of
personal and
internal
achievement.

And the moment you become
honest inside,
you will see right through it.

II. SPIRITUALITY

Questioner: What is intuition and where does it come from?

John: The intuition is a resource, a medium of expression in the outermost of consciousness. Your intuition is not your innermost being. It is only an instrument or surface vehicle. You cannot use a vehicle of expression to acquire that from which the expression originates. You cannot access your innermost through holding onto or using anything of your outermost. But the innermost can freely flow through anything of the outermost, if you allow it.

You call it a resource but where does it come from?

The intuition comes from the same place that your mind, your emotions, your will and your physical body come from. They are all surface vehicles, avenues of form for the innermost to have a place to show itself; for the innermost to express and manifest itself and you as a being. The innermost can move up into the surface vehicles of your mind, emotions, body, intuition and will, but it will be expressing everything that originates from most within, through those avenues of expression. To exist as a true human being, expressing that which is really within, within your innermost, is to express a way of being that is completely true and already complete.

Your surface vehicles are amazing means of true expression. When the innermost has something to fit into – form – then it can go into this world, move in this world and do. Your surface bodies and your life are for your innermost essence but you are accustomed to using them for yourself.

Your intuition is your capacity to pick things up in a non-mental way and also in a non-emotional way – your capacity to directly pick things up energetically. Honesty can move into the intuition and pick things up energetically, and a dishonesty of consciousness can also move into the intuition and pick things up energetically. Whatever your present way of being, that is what is sitting inside of the intuition. So the intuition is not something that is trustworthy – neither is the mind, the emotion nor the will. The only thing that is actually trustworthy is a real honesty of consciousness, nothing else.

If the ego or a self-oriented way of being is sitting inside of the intuition, then it will really need to depend on the intuition. The ego can energetically manoeuvre and ascertain what is advantageous to itself. It can also energetically pick up a threat – any disadvantage to itself. As soon as the ego picks up a disadvantage, it immediately fortifies itself, protects itself, moves into a defensive state. And when the ego through the intuition perceives that there is weakness out there, that its own energy is stronger than that weakness encountered either in a circumstance or in another person, then the ego drops its defensive position and moves into the offensive. It moves to get something and now it is not afraid.

Without the intuition the ego would not know how to move. Without the avenues of the mind, the emotion and the will, the ego would not be able to move. But you, without ego, know how to move without any of your surface vehicles. That kind of movement is honesty: consciousness allowing itself to see and realize something as it really is. It is only dishonesty of consciousness that lets itself see something as it prefers it to be, as it wishes it to be, as it needs it to be. Then seeing is conditional – it is preferential and calculated.

When there is dishonesty of consciousness, the capacity of consciousness to see reality moves into a state of semi-closure and distortion. It can be opened through focus and discipline, but that will distort the capacity for seeing and distort consciousness itself even more. What really opens that capacity and heals it is honesty: consciousness allowing itself to see what really is, without conditions, without agendas, without structures of belief, want and need.

I have been experiencing silence and then a wavering back into ego, and it seems as if it's a battle. My confusion is, why do I get lost in anger or in feeling unloved, knowing what I truly know inside?

Getting lost in those emotions occurs when there is not as much surrender taking place in you as there is knowing. What works is complete honesty. That allows you to know what is true. What has to match that equally is an absolute surrender, a kind of surrender that has no hesitation; an immediate, full, complete and intimate response to what it is that you actually, really do know is true. That allows you as consciousness to merge with truth instead of holding yourself separate from it. And you only hold yourself separate, because you know that if you merge with it, you lose everything that you are holding onto, everything that you have acquired. You lose everything that you have illegitimately merged with through hanging on.

This is as rigorous a discipline as sitting by the Ganges for ten years. It still feels like a mental process of pushing and guiding and discipline.

That is why it is not working. You cannot use your mind or your emotions or your intuition or your will, to move as a being. If you are using any aid, then what will be moving is the aid. If consciousness is using any kind of crutch, any kind of tool, then consciousness will be the tool instead of its real self. Consciousness then ceases to move purely, honestly and independently into what it really knows is true. It loses freedom of being.

When consciousness relinquishes what it is holding onto, lets go of using a tool in an attempt to move as a being, then a movement of true consciousness happens. That movement is a natural and clean flow of consciousness that has no use of will in it; there is no effort, just a clarity and an evenness of being.

When there is not an honesty – when there is not a surrender to what consciousness knows is true, when you as consciousness move inside of your mental, volitional, intuitional or emotional vehicles – you are doing so because of desiring control and desiring something that the real you does not need. It is consciousness using restriction to create movement for a self-created agenda. The only reason that consciousness would use restriction through the surface vehicles to create movement, is to restrict something, to confine, limit and control something. But consciousness ends up being trapped. In wishing to restrict, consciousness is then trapped by restriction. The more consciousness uses the quality of that restriction to try to unrestrict – to go home to the true, unrestricted way of pure being – the deeper it drops into the restriction.

The moment consciousness is unconditionally okay with being restricted in any possible way that presently exists, completely lets go into being okay restricted, confined or trapped without that condition ever needing change, then consciousness simply is in a state of unrestriction. Restriction no longer confines, because then consciousness is inside of restriction in a way that is genuinely and warmly okay. Inside that depth of okayness there is no restriction.

So now, instead of restriction being inside of consciousness, there has been a replacement by absolute okayness inside of consciousness. What remains is only a perceived restriction in the surface vehicles that surround consciousness. And consciousness has actually gone home to a true way of being, simply by being unconditionally okay with all the restriction, as is.

It is difficult to drop the mental habits and understand what it is to let consciousness unfold with no restrictions.

It is not difficult unless it is something that you do not honestly want to do. Then it is difficult. You cannot do something that you do not want to do. If you are hanging onto something and you do not really want to let go of it, then trying to let go of it is grabbing even stronger. If all of what you are is just simply okay with letting something go, then in that very moment there is an opening, there is a softening, there is a letting-go without even trying. There is no effort, no energy used in letting-go. You are just being what you really are. You are being in your natural state which will take you from holding to being. And if it is difficult from here to there, it is only because you are wanting to be here. You are not really wanting to be there, in that true way of being. You do not want to let go. If you are trying to let go and it is difficult, what is confronted is your own lack of honesty. That is what is in question.

What is being made manifest is consciousness in a state of inner conflict. Part of consciousness hungers to let go, yearns to let go, only because that is what is true. And another part of consciousness is hanging on, only because it wants to. It still perceives and trusts its own thoughts, its own feelings; it trusts that there is some advantage to hanging onto a particular emotion, ideal or thought. It will not let go because there is hope invested in what it is hanging onto. Hope that someday, sometime, it will get what it is looking for, get what it is expecting through that hanging on.

The moment the measure of consciousness that is hanging on becomes honest, it begins to see that what it is doing is in a way of being that is untrue. It is being incongruent with itself to be in a state of holding. And the moment it begins to let go – the moment it becomes okay with no longer needing to hold, to trust in something that is merely a perception, to trust what it knows is true in a way of being that is open and soft – then internal conflict ends. Now all of consciousness is like this. When consciousness is completely honest like that and then tries to hang onto something, it cannot; it is unable to. Consciousness in complete honesty does not have the capacity to hang on.

The only way a hanging on can take place, is for consciousness in some tiny little way to become dishonest. Then holding on is instantaneous and letting-go is an impossibility. Dishonest consciousness cannot let go. If you are having difficulty in surrendering, it is because part of you does not want to. When that part becomes honest it will instinctively, by nature, without any effort, love letting-go.

Thousands of years ago people just retreated to caves, but I have come to realize that the truth for me isn't like the enlightenment consciousness from thousands of years ago. The blending of spirituality and humanity is what is true for me. I am referring to a kind of spirituality that comes from having time in retreat so that I can really find myself and be in truth. My challenge is blending that with daily life, like raising teenagers.

When consciousness is being honest — remains completely surrendered to a way of openness and softness and innermost vulnerability that lives only to serve what it knows is true, instead of what it would like to be true for any reason — then it does not matter what it does in this life. It does not matter how it chooses or which way it goes, it cannot miss at all in anything, ever. You do not need any kind of prescribed way of choosing or any prescribed way of doing. You do not need any kind of structure or code or workable way of doing things, you just simply could not miss.

If there is dishonesty of consciousness, then there is a perceived need of structure: a code, ways of doing things that become right and wrong, ways of doing that are better. Then consciousness becomes opinionated. You become self-righteous, you become judgmental, you become a real somebody who has something. And there will always be someone else who is higher, and there will always be someone else who is lower. It will not matter what you touch and what you do, nothing in life, including spirituality, will ever work at all. Where there is dishonesty, it will poison everything you touch, taint everything you try. It will ruin everything and that is good, because then as consciousness you do not get away with anything. If things are not working for you inside, that is wonderful.

You mentioned how the ego reaches out to control. If you are around someone who is doing that and you feel unloved because of that, and the anger is there, is that good?

Anger is a massive disqualifier. The moment there is anger, your way of being is totally disqualified. Whatever it is that you think you are doing that is spiritual or right or clean or the best, has no value if anger is allowed to arise from it. It is all a waste, all for nothing; there is nothing there that is redeemable. Everything you are believing to be right or clean, that you actually do not know to be right or clean from a place of innermost openness and softness, is only worth being totally replaced.

That's a big red flag when it comes up.

What dishonesty will do when that red flag comes up, is turn in on itself and work with the anger. That work is equally totally useless. It never works. If it happens to seem to work, you will become self-righteous: you have become one who knows how to work with anger, you have dealt with your own anger, you are really "somebody" now. Now you will want to change everyone else who has anger. You will want to show them. You will want to change them and if they do not agree with your way, you will become frustrated. You will again become angry.

Working with anything inside, if there is not an absolute honesty and surrender, does not work. It only gets worse. Spiritual work is a lie. If you take off the mask of doing spiritual work, what is behind it is: "What do I get out of this? I want something here, and I want it my way." Doing spiritual work is based on a fundamental, inner non-acceptance of things as they presently are. Doing spiritual work is based on not-okayness. It is based on the illusion that you need to change, and it is based on the illusion that you are able to change fundamentally, which you are not. Have you ever really changed yourself inside, ever, in your entire life? You can make behavioural adjustments, but they have nothing to do with what you are as a being.

We dress up our behaviour, like anger, until it becomes more subtle but it's still there.

You cannot change your patterns of behaviour. But you can allow your way of being to change by instantaneously and effortlessly letting that dishonesty soften and open up, by allowing consciousness to be honest. That is profound and real change. That is the only true change you are capable of, nothing else.

To work on yourself is to use some kind of hanging on, to use the energy of hanging on to do something inside of you. What you will actually be doing is a deeper, more meaningful hanging on. There is nothing to change inside of you. There is nothing to do, nothing that you can change, nothing inside that you actually have need of. Anything that you perceive you want or need, you do not. And the moment you become honest inside, you know it is true. Mixing spiritual work with anything is mixing internal effort with everything. That makes everything worse.

That sounds so good, to try to bring spirituality or spirit into the human situation.

Why would you ever want to bring spirituality into the human situation? What would be your agenda? Why would you want to do that?

To uplift, to make things better.

Why would you ever want to uplift anything and make anything better? Why would you want to help anyone in any way you think or feel they should be helped? Why would you ever want to help yourself, and trust that your perceptions, based on your own personal feelings, thoughts and agendas, will show you what needs to be done? Why would you want to bring about betterment, especially the meaningful kind? Only to get something that you do not need. It is only done to get something more of what in reality, in the innermost of consciousness, you do not need at all. That is why it never works, why it is never true to do spiritual work of any kind.

All spiritual work, in the absence of absolute honesty and surrender, can be nothing other than a lie. It is a core distraction from honesty, a distraction from surrender, a distraction into some form of personal and internal achievement. It is the need to be a somebody who has something. There is no good reason for spiritual work: not one. We make reasons up. But with just a little bit of honesty we can see right through them.

The only right that you have is to be completely honest with everything, as is. That works. Anyone who has an agenda to love and to help and to serve is poisonous. There is already a state of delusion, of actually believing that there is something internally that needs to be done. That person is already believing that he or she is capable of doing it.

A little baby is in it. There is a flow of love, and yet there is no agenda to love. The moment there is an agenda to love for any reason at all, what is inside is no longer clean. The only reason that you could ever have an agenda to love is to get something out of it. There is not an issue anywhere in this world, that existed at any time ever in history, that has ever been worth living for – ever. There is no such thing as a worthwhile issue, not of any kind, for any reason. To live for an issue requires a personal agenda. To live for an issue requires the support of personalized reasons that have nothing to do with honesty or truth. Those reasons have only to do with getting something, with doing something that does not, in reality, need to be done.

If you are living for any kind of issue, then by virtue of that, you have become violent. Your way of being has become one of unnatural force and vehemence originating from emotional or mental agitation, instead of from the natural state of rest of a true way of being. If you have an issue, and if there is anything that frustrates that issue, you will experience a constriction. That constriction is the birthplace of anger. The anger has not shown yet. It is not until the someone or the something frustrating the issue that you are holding onto stays there long enough for the constriction to worsen that you will finally be unable to contain it. You will manifest the constriction in reaction, because you cannot have what it is that you want. You are not getting your way. And that is violence. It is living for any issue of any kind.

But what you honestly know is true is a way of being that is worth living for. That way is worth giving your entire self-created existence to: your past, your present, your future, your surface vehicles, your agendas, your issues, your whole life – everything. You can rightly live in total devotion, using all that you are, to the tiniest little bit that from a place of innermost honesty you know to be true. You can turn over your whole life to that little bit.

But to give any part of you, to give any energy at all to anything other than what you honestly know is true, then you are in a place that you do not belong. You are functioning away from a way of being that is true. You are doing something that is untrue, making something matter that does not matter. And those things that really do matter of the littlest bit that you actually know is true, you have made not matter by covering up and creating something else. What you are really saying is: "This matters, this really matters to me, this matters enough that I will actually live for this." Spirituality and any kind of agenda taken to heart are deadly. They are poisonous to a true way of being and they distort everything they touch.

Consciousness allowing itself to open up and be honest all the way through – allowing the integrity of what it actually does know is true, to be of supreme value – that is consciousness being alive and in flow. That kind of consciousness could do anything in this life, and it would never miss, it could not miss. But being spiritual, that is just a sophisticated way of stealing. The only reason one would ever be spiritual is to get something. It has nothing to do with giving into what one honestly knows is true, because then all that would remain in consciousness would be honesty and surrender.

If only honesty and surrender remained, there would be a flow from the innermost moving all the way through consciousness, through all of the surface vehicles, moving and washing through everything in this world, everything in this life. Everything touched by that flow would heal, would be given life. And there would be no agenda to it. And none of this would be happening for a reason. It would just simply be a flow of truth right from the innermost. There would be no trying.

Consciousness would naturally flow, just like a baby, just like a flower. A flower makes no effort being what it is, when it touches you in the way that it touches you. A little baby you are holding, who is looking inside of you and knowing you, makes no effort; there is an absence of trying to do anything. But there is such an awesome flow, unlike with spiritual people.

Spiritual people are incurably judgmental, incurably self-righteous, incurable somebodies who have something; they are incurably important. And there is only one thing in the whole universe, one thing in all of consciousness that can possibly heal something that is distorted: honesty. Honesty pierces right through distortion and makes manifest what really is. Honesty is the only thing that can get inside and crack distortion open. Absolutely anything else only makes it worse.

If there is any identity at all in being spiritual – in being a loving person, helpful, tender, gentle, considerate, thoughtful, open-minded or soft – any identity at all, then that softness, gentleness, openness, spirituality, lovingness or tenderness is only a mask, covering a presence interested only in achieving or acquiring something.

When something is real, when something actually comes from the innermost and is allowed to come all the way to the surface and be as is, then there will be love. There will be tenderness and there will be gentleness. There will be so many different kinds of expression of being that are all in flow. And in all the ways this flow could manifest itself, be in this life and express itself, there would be no identity in them at all; the flow would just be what it is. But there would be awareness of the kind of flow taking place. There would be awareness, if there is love for example, but no identity in being a loving person. There would be awareness of a flow of helpfulness, tenderness or thoughtfulness, but no identity in being helpful, thoughtful or tender. True flow like that could never come from a somebody, because only a nobody would allow that kind of flow to manifest.

Our families or others said to us "you're nice," or "you're gentle" and we believed it. Is that how it started?

That is how it started. We believed it, but not because someone said it. We believed it, because what someone said was convenient to what we were already looking for. As consciousness, we used that person, used that person's words.

At one point there was an innocence of being, but because of pain, because of some kind of suffering in one of your surface vehicles, you as consciousness began to wonder if there was something that you could do; if you could do something outside of yourself, inside of one of your surface vehicles – in your mind, in your emotions – to protect yourself from the pain.

When you were being honest, when you checked inside in the place of knowing, it was wonderfully and abundantly clear that there was nothing that needed to be done. As the pain was there, everything inside of consciousness knew that it was so okay. There was nothing that needed to change.

But consciousness looked at that and decided: "That's not good enough, it's not good enough that everything is so okay, not good enough that the pain is really, really okay, because that does not stop the pain. I am going to move outward; I believe there is something that I can do to stop the pain." But consciousness knew within, that there was nothing that needed to be done. It chose to believe something that it actually knew was not true. So it extended itself as consciousness into the surface vehicles in search of a way of gaining control over the pain; protecting itself from something that it did not need to be protected from, helping something inside of consciousness that was already presently, wonderfully complete.

When that sort of consciousness, out there reaching, hears a parent say "you're special," and that consciousness hears it inside of the emotional vehicle, so that any pain within the emotional vehicle is at that moment replaced by the good feeling of being told "you're special," then that consciousness is feeling better within the emotional body. It is not actually better inside, but it has a feeling of betterment. That consciousness says: "I can work with this, maybe I can get more," and it begins to live for the emotional attachment to happiness and the desire for pain relief. Consciousness that has moved out of itself in that way becomes more and more deeply entrenched in the emotional vehicle, the mental vehicle, the intuitional vehicle; caught in them, trapped in them, held inside of a self-created world far away from what it really is. Consciousness does that long enough until it realizes: "I am lost. Where am I? I don't know who I am. I don't know what is true. What is going on? Nothing is working. Nothing at all is working."

Now consciousness is on a path, a path to find its way back to a way that is complete and perfect. And consciousness, through the mind, calls that enlightenment and awakening. And as long as it is in need of awakening, in need of enlightenment, in need of pain relief or anything at all, then the search for truth continues. But truth is not really what that consciousness is looking for at all. It is looking to feel good, looking for comfort and for pain relief. Consciousness calls it "looking for truth" or calls it a search, but it is lying to itself. Consciousness has become a spiritual liar instead of just a plain liar, and it gets worse and worse and worse.

Everything consciousness touches from that way of being never works. It can adjust so many things and it can appear to change things, but it cannot change its internal state. It is not until consciousness, from far away from home, completely lets go of ever needing to get home; when it lets itself be unconditionally okay in a state where there is anger, frustration, greed, selfishness and the many ugly things that are caught inside of itself, that consciousness finally finds itself in a state of absolute, warm okayness. That is consciousness simply being what it is, as is.

All that remains is rest: a warm flow of total and complete acceptance, the kind of acceptance where there is nothing that ever,

ever again needs to change. And without consciousness realizing what is happening within the mental, emotional and intuitional vehicles, its way of being from outermost consciousness now matches a way of being that is of the innermost. And because there is a match in a way of being between the outermost and the innermost of consciousness, there is an instantaneous return home to reality, to truth.

Consciousness is now whole and complete. It is home in a true way of being, and it did not do anything to change. The entire path ended. Ever needing to change ended. Needing to fix something ended. The want and desire of needing anything good or relieving anything bad ended. Every kind of internal doing is finally and completely over.

Now there is a way of being that is actually true. There is unconditional okayness, as is. You are home. And that is how easy it is. That is how healing it is. All that happened was just total honesty and a surrender to what consciousness actually knew was true. Consciousness became awakened; it went home. It returned to what really, really is, without mentally, emotionally and intuitionally even realizing what was taking place.

How does that happen?

How does consciousness away from home be in a way that is true? It does that by being honest, by letting-go of being loyal to a perception, to a thought, to a want, a need, an emotion, an ideal. It is when consciousness finally lets go of being true to anything other than what it actually and honestly knows is true. If you have any kind of issue with anything in this life, you are being true to something that is not true. You are being true to a perception, an illusion, a lie, and you are not being true to that littlest bit that you actually know is true. You have covered up that little bit, because each time you see it, you know that being true to it would mean losing your issues. You would be losing your self-created dreams and desires. You would lose living inside of all of that. You would not get what you want anymore – you would lose control.

So then you quickly cover up that tiny little bit that you know is true. You seal it off so that you cannot even stumble over it, because it is far too dangerous; that tiny little bit can unravel your whole life! And once that is sealed off, you quiet that little voice by standing on top of it. You have laboured to shut it out. You can no longer hear it, and now you feel safe.

Now you go about looking for a personal truth that is worth living for, one that satisfies you, one that is really good for you. You look for some kind of issue that you can live for, that will make you happy, make you a somebody; an issue that you can climb up inside of as consciousness to look the way that you want to look, be what you want to be. You do it all for you. It may look as though you are doing it for selfless reasons or for someone else, but you are doing it only for you. And that is so easily exposed. Just take the mask, crack it open, take a peek inside and see what is underneath. If someone touches that mask and frustrates it, begins to pull it off, you will be severely threatened. Your held together identity and agenda are covering a reality you cannot afford to expose.

I am feeling that I don't trust that I actually know what that core truth really is.

Then you have it easy. If you do not trust that you know, then you do not have to believe any of your opinions, ideals, hopes, wants, needs and dreams. You will not trust those, because you know that you do not trust yourself. So instantly, all of that no longer matters and now you are relieved; all of your burdens are gone.

It is actually nourishing, because it resonates with your innermost being. When you hear it, your innermost being moves up within you and loves what you are hearing. It does not do that with your issues. Your innermost being never participates with your issues or with your spirituality. It cannot, because it knows there is nothing there. When you hear this, you love it, because your being loves it. It is relieving, because it is what you have always known to be true. It is so healing. The healing works, the nourishment works; the words give you a space inside where you can totally let go and settle, a space inside where you are actually allowed to lay your head, and there is nothing more to do. There is rest inside, there is room enough to be.

What will happen is that your mind – consciousness within the mind – will realize some of the implications of what you are hearing and some of the implications of what you are letting in. And when you realize those implications, as you begin to see how they will spread out through your life through your emotional and your mental vehicle and your will, realize the implications of losing everything that you are holding onto, then you will see them mapped out over your entire life. You will realize that you will lose all of what you have held onto, and it is then that you may begin to hesitate. Consciousness begins to evaluate: "Is it worth it, is it worth losing that much to be inside of what I know is true?" And it starts to become anxious, starts to become concerned. It is already leaning toward hanging onto everything, because the loss is too profound, too great. And then dishonesty, bit by bit, begins to climb back in and reinstate itself. And then the ego comes back together and says: "That was close!"

How do you keep that from happening?

Let yourself be warmly okay and unconditionally okay with every form of not-okayness that you ever encounter again. Then it will be easy. As soon as there is something that you perceive ought to be changed or is internally important to change, you can instead allow a new and living response inside to warmly and unconditionally accept the issue, just as is. There is no need to participate in changing anything. Then you are left warmly okay; a true, living acceptance within any kind of circumstance, every kind of not-okayness.

I get a sense of the isolation that would arise from that because there is going to be a lot of not-okayness around. People won't like that.

There are a whole lot of not-okay people around you. And if you let yourself be unconditionally okay with everything as is, that will expose them. They may at first be warmly drawn to be just like you, but that may make them angry, if they do not truly want to be okay, if they want and they insist on being not-okay. So you may begin to lose your friends.

The other possibility is that anyone around you who is hungering for reality, will irresistibly be drawn to just simply be with you. There will be something about your space that will actually draw them to lay their head, and they may not even know what in the world you are talking about. They may not comprehend what you are doing, but they will love what you are. The way you are will be nourishment to them. It will be healing to them, and there will be an attraction of being to be just like you. And you did not even try to love them or help them or change them. It all happened effortlessly. Honesty and surrender truly work.

I wonder if self-love is a good label for that acceptance of what is not-okay?

Effort and self-love will only wound you more. If there is any effort in it, any at all, then you are just contorting yourself as consciousness. You are just beating yourself up within, trying to do something that from a place of inner honesty, you are not interested in at all.

Only an effortless being gentle with yourself, an effortless giving space for yourself to just simply be, works. Bringing in any kind of energy to ascertain or protect that space, to have your "all I want to do is just be" space, is just a delusion. If there is any effort, then it is another distraction, something else that will not work.

A genuine loving yourself is a warm letting-go of needing to love yourself. It is a relinquishing of effort to hold yourself together or try to love yourself. A genuine loving yourself is not something to do, when looking for comfort has not worked and nothing else so far has either. When there is an integrity right from your innermost being all the way through to the outermost – a natural and effortless being gentle with yourself — that works. But if there is any tiny little kink in it because of an emotional pull to being gentle with yourself for a feel-good, then it will self-destruct. It will not work.

As soon as there is a tiny compromise of integrity from within all the way through to the outermost — a compromise of an integrity of being through trusting a thought, a perception, an emotion, an external pressure, a want or a need, anything other than what you actually know is true — then there is a tiny letting in of dishonesty. And that will ruin everything you touch and do. But if a simple purity of response is allowed to move through consciousness, all the way to the outermost, and you will not compromise that simple knowing for pain relief, or the achievement of enlightenment or happiness, not for anything at all, then everything of that simple, pure response moving through you, that comes from your innermost, works. It heals, it nourishes. You will be loving and enjoying yourself without even trying. In every kind of flow that moves through you, there will never be any effort attached to it at all.

So that means that any kind of spiritual work is a lie? That sounds great because I am tired of spiritual work.

Everyone is.

What do you think of what I call, "spiritual play?" It is not trying to force yourself into something, but rather letting yourself learn more to flow.

That is less painful, but that is still not it, because that play can be frustrated. It is embedded in the playfulness. Why would you do spiritual play? If it is just play, why would you choose spiritual play, why not choose another kind of play?

Because you realize that just being and following the flow of certain deeds is spiritual; not because you're trying to be spiritual and not because you're judging how spiritual it is. It's a type of acceptance.

There can be a measure of reality within the acceptance, but what would be your reason for moving into that state?

Because it feels right.

What if moving into a state of acceptance because it feels right, were to slowly make everything worse? Would you still do the "acceptance play?"

That would be the time to move on. If it happened to me, I would certainly watch for that.

It can happen when true acceptance goes deep, that it makes you feel not very good. Deep within are the things that you have been holding down under pressure, that you did not under any circumstance ever allow yourself to see because they cut too deeply, hurt too much or threatened you to the core. For there to be a profound acceptance, for you to take your hands off something that you did not want to see and for you to warmly accept it, then painful and distressing things could come up from within you that you have been holding down for a very long time. When these are given room to actually come inside of your mental, emotional, physical, intuitional and volitional vehicles because of your state of acceptance, it could appear as though you are fast regressing, and that life is getting worse.

If the only reason that there is an acceptance is just because that is what you know is true, and if you surrender to that and your life begins to worsen, will you stay in that acceptance? Or will you stop because your life is getting worse? When you seem to be getting worse instead of better, will you abandon what you know and trust your perceptions that something must be wrong? Will you then stop the openness, softness and acceptance and move into a space of evaluation?

I think I have enough of a glimpse of what that is, and I get far enough into that, but part of being truthful is to say I am not ready to be fully truthful. And for me to realize that about myself has been part of that extreme acceptance process. It only goes so far and then it stalls.

What is the acceptance working for, you or your innermost being? Does the acceptance you are describing work well for your being? Does your way of doing things inside work so well for your being that it clears the whole space of you so that your being has room to come up within you and occupy that space, go anywhere inside of that space, go anywhere in your present life, past and future and do anything that it is moved to do? Does your "acceptance" exist only to accommodate your being? Are you in total devotion to your being in such a way that you would give it anything that it moved toward? If your being moved you to let go of something, would you instantly acquiesce with that and surrender and let go? Do you live for it and no longer live for you? If your acceptance is truly that way, then what you are doing is for your being.

If the acceptance is for you, then the letting-go within the acceptance gives you more space; it clears space inside for you to be more comfortable, because then there is less stress. When the measure to which you are holding onto something is reduced, there will be less stress inside and more comfort. And there is enough genius of consciousness to immediately recognize that. You realize that opening and softening, letting-go, surrendering – even honesty, if you use it in the right measure – can in some way give you what you want. It will all work to achieve just enough comfort, but don't let in too much honesty, because then everything will be replaced. Then your being will come in and it will take over, it will replace you and you do not want that to happen. So you learn how far to go. You have a line drawn inside; you will not be more honest than a certain amount, because more than that costs too much.

II. SPIRITUALITY

What I need is to be around people who are living more honestly and to feel directly inspired by that way you described, rather than being what I am.

For you to be around someone who lives that way, a pull, an attraction of being, a hunger of being occurs. That pull is there because your being is coming out of you, leaving you behind and preferring to be with that person rather than in you. That is why it causes a pull. And when that happens within you, it does something to you. There is a resonance of truth flowing through you and moving you. That flow of truth is there because it is an attraction of being, an attraction from within you as consciousness to the beingness outside of you. And you can either surrender to that flow and that pull of being, be with that flow as is, that is moving from within toward something outside of you, or you can hold out on your own.

If you decide you will not flow in something like that, unless the flow gets to go to you, gets to be about you instead of about something outside of you that your being recognizes as truer than you, then you hold out. And as soon as you hold out, then you become more and more non-accepting of that flow of being, that pull of being. Then you will not go to where that pull occurs. You will not hang around that person anymore, because that kind of flow is interrupting your life.

But if that flow to you is healing – if that pull moves you, because your being is moving through you and out toward something that is in a way of being just like itself; if that in any way heals or pulls or touches or satisfies as it moves through you – then you will begin to give into it a little bit. You will begin to give up those things that you are hanging onto, and that flow will become stronger and stronger. It will become insatiable; you will end up turning into, end up becoming just like that other being who you are hanging around. And that will happen, because your own being is being just like that. Your being is always being just like that; you have just let yourself side with its flow. Then an internal merge happens. You become your being.

Why would I want to do that?

Why would you acquiesce with your being, acquiesce with the flow that comes from your innermost being?

What is different about the attraction to that and the attraction of the outer, if I am free from all needs and wants?

If you are free from all needs and wants and there is a flow of being that moves right through you, if your being is going toward something outside of you and you are free of all attachment, then you would without effort become one with that flow. You would join that preference of being, and you would naturally go where your being is going.

That being that is free of attachment might be equally attracted to me though.

But if your being is going that way, toward the other being, it is because there is something there that is causing a pull. If it were the other way around, that being would come to you.

Why do you do these talks?

It is a response of being, a movement of being. There is a love of being that moves me to knock on everyone's door. No one needs to open, ever. I just do what it is that I am so much in love with, that originates from my innermost. I do what I am moved to do from a depth of innermost consciousness, from a way of complete and absolute surrender to that true way of being. And there is an integrity of response that goes all the way through, that has no condition attached to it. That is why I do what I do.

Do you stay in the state of internal coherence that you described, with no kinks in the flow from the innermost to the outermost, in honesty, one hundred

II. SPIRITUALITY

percent of the time, or is this a thing that comes on and off?

It is continuous because that is all that I am in love with. That is what I am intimate with. I have no other treasure. Regarding anything else, I am empty.

Those who have spent time with you, they may not able to do that one hundred percent of the time, but are able to do that only part of the time?

There are very, very few who can do it all the time with a groundedness and a natural constancy, and there are many more who can live in it in a way that is fragile, like a tiny little child first learning how to ride a bicycle, sort of "all over the place." It looks like that child could run into almost anything, but he or she is doing it, it is happening. There is a living internal coherence, and there is nothing untrue supporting it. There are many in that way of being.

What about relationship? Where does that fit into this?

That does not fit in anywhere, not until you are home. Until you are home, you do not fit into anything that is real.

When people are real and they are home, they do have relationships. Why?

When there is a response of being to be in a relationship – not for mental, emotional, sexual, intuitional or volitional reasons; not for reasons that have anything to do with this whole life but just for an innermost reason; a pull and a response, a movement of being – then what forms is a relationship of being. If there is nothing of consciousness that illegitimately attaches to it through the surface vehicles, then that relationship of being forms and forms. A base begins to form, a foundation in which two beings can be home together without the need of any mental, emotional, sexual, intuitional or volitional help to make it better.

A base of being develops that becomes so solid that all the surface vehicles can legitimately be drawn by beingness into that base, and those surface vehicles will never be greater than the base. They will never exceed the capacity for expression that the base itself has created or become. The surface vehicles become progressively more integrated and incorporated into beingness. And they are not used for anything other than for the being to flow through and to express itself. That is the only real reason for relationships.

How do non-volitional expressions of inner being look externally? How do people know they are not deluding themselves, not still serving a deeper form of ego agenda?

The easiest way to tell is if there is any identity in it at all.

So, for example, if one of the people that you spend time with had an identity as being enlightened, then obviously that would be one of those kinks that was slipping in.

If any of them were to touch that, then everyone else whose awareness is so opened up that they could see it, would become very warmly humoured with what they saw. In the warmest way, they would see right through it, without judgment. When humour comes right from the very innermost, it is the best. It is the only kind of humour that truly heals and nourishes. I just love seeing what they see. They are watching someone who is wearing a process of enlightenment.

I like the humorous part of this.

CHAPTER 3

Innermost – Outermost

Nothing that is true or real
can ever be lost.
You cannot damage reality.
Your innermost is made of it –
it is that.

Your innermost is incorruptible:
it cannot be defiled,
it cannot be distorted.
There is no cheating, no trickery that works.
The only thing of the outermost
that has access to the innermost,
is a way of being that is true.

When that way of being
matches the innermost way,
then without any effort,
without any construct,
the outermost can dwell in the innermost,
and the innermost can express itself
freely
through the outermost.

Now there is wholeness –
completeness of consciousness.
And it is as good
as you always knew it to be,
as beautiful
as you always knew it to be.
It is the way that is true.

III. INNERMOST - OUTERMOST

Questioner: I don't know how to be. It seems like the most honest thing for me to do is dig the earth and bury myself in it. In that way I'll be serving my being, because I don't know how to be. It seems like then I can't be betraying my being, I can't continue being dishonest and disillusioned.

John: What is it that you are trying to be? What does it respond to? What does it thrive on, what does it love? And all of this has nothing to do with you; you are not a part of this. We are just talking about it. What does it thrive on? What makes it live? What moves it?

I have such a resistance to saying the word.

Do you know your being? Since you have nothing to do with this, your resistance does not count.

Well, it's absolute truth.

And those are not just words; you know the taste of that. The only reason you have resistance in using those words, is because you have heard them used so often. People have spoken them so many times, but there was nothing of reality there.

When I said to you I don't know how to be, I meant I don't know how to give space to my being.

When you let your way be determined by the way of your being, that gives space to your being.

In moment to moment living, I don't know how that happens or how that is done.

You do not have to. You do not need to know or understand moment to moment. Is there any moment, any moment at all that you know how to give space to your being?

There have been moments. But I don't know if I gave space to my being or whether it just kind of happened.

Your being never creates space in you because you are the holder of power, not it. The place of weakness is always within your being. Your being holds no power. All it is, is what is true. Your being is functioning as living truth, but it is not using any power.

There have been those moments. I felt it was just like a gift that came my way rather than me participating in some way.

The only reason that you could have been gifted by something from your being is because within you there was a presence of receiving rather than of taking. The receiving was not for you; there was receiving, because it was true to receive. You were gifted with something that you knew was absolutely true. And you loved it. You loved it more than you.

That's why I don't want to betray it. I think that when I am with people I betray it. So if I am alone there is less likelihood of betraying it.

When there is a sensitivity to your being, and you see yourself betraying it all the time around other people, then you are betraying it through your own self-created patterns of thought and emotion, want and need. Then, as quickly as you betray it, you get to soften in the midst of realizing what it is that you have just betrayed. It does not matter if you have betrayed your being.

But it does matter.

Only to you, the you that you are accustomed to identifying yourself as.

III. INNERMOST - OUTERMOST

Doesn't it matter to the being?

No, it does not matter to your being as long as the moment you realize it, you respond to it instead of to you.

But in that moment when I realize it, I don't know whether I am responding to it or to me. Just the knowing that I have betrayed it doesn't mean that I respond to it.

There are two ways of being that you know. There is one way that closes, tightens, constricts, hardens, insists, demands and says no or says a conditional yes. And the other way of being that you know opens, softens and lets go. It will be moldable, warmly moldable, responsive and non-reactive. Those are the only two ways of being that you know.

While you clearly know one way of being to be untrue, the other way of being you clearly know to be wonderfully true. Then, when you see yourself betraying your being, you can let yourself move into a way of being that you know is true. You can let go of needing to get it right. You can let go of needing to be no longer a betrayer of your being. It is letting yourself be warmly and unconditionally okay in realizing that you are a betrayer of your being.

It's hard because I have betrayed my being for so long.

When there is a warm acceptance that what you are is a betrayer of your being, then all of your sensitivity which has been closed for so long begins to open up. You will no longer be hard on yourself. What will happen is that your heart will begin to break, because you will realize that your being is very tenderly okay with you having betrayed it. Your being only waits to have any kind of space to simply come up through your consciousness from the innermost and just be with you. The fact that you have betrayed it does not matter to your being. Your being is ever present to acquiesce with your space, and it does not matter what you have done to it.

Isn't the being fragile?

Your innermost is not fragile. The amount of your innermost being that has come into form in terms of the real you, that is fragile. The real you has not been given very much of a chance in living your life.

To realize that you have betrayed your being is a wonderful realization. It is a kind of realization that, when you fully let it in, melts everything. If you completely let in the realization that you have betrayed your own being, it will make you as tender as your own being. It will make you as soft as your own being. Then you will be just like it. Then you are being that, instead of you. Then you are being the real you instead of the you that you are accustomed to only it does not happen in a way that you would ever think, or ever feel.

You can never go by your thoughts and feelings to tell you what is happening in terms of truth and the real you. Your thoughts and your feelings cannot be your guides. Then as consciousness you will be giving up your trust in thoughts and feelings to know yourself and to know what is true. The knowing of truth precedes thoughts and feelings. The knowing of truth does not come from thoughts and feelings. But the knowing of truth can really be expressed through thoughts and feelings.

When there are no thoughts or feelings and there is just a blank, nothingness, is that a kind of space for truth?

When there are no thoughts, no feelings, but there is a warm, fulfilling, satisfying space that neither your mind, emotions nor intuition can comprehend or identify, then you as consciousness are in a state of outer stillness. While you happen to be in a state of outer stillness where there is no identifiable movement in your surface vehicles at all, it is simply inner stillness moving all the way through the surface vehicles and expressing itself outwardly.

You can allow that same inner stillness of being to be there in the midst of the outer turmoil of self-created mental, emotional, intuitional and volitional patterns of behaviour as well. The space of stillness inside or the way of being inside is the same in both situations. But when there is outer turmoil, the stillness is more like a state of inner not needing to do, and not needing to escape in the midst of all the outer movement surrounding you.

I tend to think that I want to be burned up completely.

For your being? Or for pain relief?

If I am burned up completely, then my being has more of a chance.

What if your innermost being does not mind if you are there? What if it does not matter to your being if you are there, just as long as you are not trusting you? While you are not trusting you, then to your being it does not matter at all that you are there. For you to wish that the you you have created be burned up so that your being could have space, that would grieve your being, because it is not wanting that. Your innermost being does not thrive in you being burned up, it thrives in you giving yourself away.

But if all that gets burned up is not real anyway? It's spoken about as being worthless: what does it matter if it gets burned up, because it doesn't serve any purpose?

It does serve a purpose. It is really you. It is the part of consciousness that is the holder of power, the holder of choice. Your innermost being is not the holder of choice.

Can't I give choice to my being? I think I am here because I want to give that choice to my being.

And you perceive that the you you are used to, if you could just obliterate it, would leave more space for your being? There would not be more space. Then that part of consciousness – the holder of choice that was only identifying with the you that you have created and that you are accustomed to – that part of consciousness would also be obliterated. And now, where would your innermost being have to go, to be? It would have no place for expression.

You cannot obliterate consciousness. But consciousness can cease trusting a you that it thinks it is, but actually knows it is not. The only burning up that is worth taking place is the burning up of what you have been trusting. Then, the only thing that dies is an old way of trusting, an illegitimate trust. All that dies is consciousness trusting that the mental and the emotional bodies or vehicles are some kind of reliable mirror in which the reflection it sees is itself. But it is not. The only reflection that consciousness is seeing is the reflection of thoughts and feelings. So it is not about obliterating the surface bodies or vehicles.

When you say "surface body" you don't mean the physical, do you?

I am referring to the burning up of an illusion. All that you lose, all that is burned up, is an illegitimate trust in something other than what you know, to tell you what is true. When you are honest, you know that nothing outside of that knowing can tell you what is true at all – it only tells you what you are thinking and feeling. So now, instead of trusting what you are thinking and feeling in any of your surface vehicles to tell you what is true, you can begin to trust the littlest bit that you presently know is true.

The very simplest knowing is that of opening and softening and letting-go. When you know you are hanging onto something inside, the simplest knowing is to just let it go. It does not matter how that makes you feel, it does not matter what you are thinking, it does not matter what you are experiencing and going through. In the midst of all of that, what you know is let it go.

I've heard you say also that it's easy.

You do not have to let go through your mind. If it were through your mind, it would be really, really difficult.

It's not through the mind, it's not through the emotions, not through the will or whatever else there is. So is it through something that is deeper?

It is through you. It is only you as consciousness who can let go. And consciousness does not need the mind or the will to do it. The will does not help. When consciousness is trusting and using the will to let go, then consciousness is trying to let go. Consciousness can let go of needing to use the will to let go. Then the first thing to let go of, is trying.

Doesn't consciousness know that I want to let go?

But you see, you are that. It is you who are consciousness. Consciousness is not something tucked away inside of you, that you cannot seem to access. You are that. And consciousness can be honest. Then it sees, and it knows itself.

Consciousness can also be dishonest. Consciousness can say: "I need such and such to be true." And as soon as consciousness lets in a want and a need, then immediately that measure of consciousness rushes into all the surface vehicles and all the resources, pulls together the means of creating whatever it is that it wants and needs, and manifests that inside. Now you have something that seems real. To you as consciousness it only seems real.

But that is a reality based only on thoughts and feelings. As soon as that dishonesty of consciousness is allowed to be just a little bit gentled and quieted, immediately it begins to realize that this reality that seems so real, has nothing in it – there is no depth to it. There is really nothing there. There are thoughts and feelings, but there is nothing real in them. There is no resonance of being. There is nothing that your innermost of consciousness rises up and responds to, because the innermost of consciousness will only respond to something in the outermost of consciousness that is of the same way of being.

So if the outermost of consciousness, which has all the power, is holding onto a belief or a want or a need for something to be true, then there will be a way of being in the outermost that is different from the innermost of consciousness. And the innermost will not participate with what the outermost is presently holding onto. That is because the way of being, in that holding on, is different than the way of being of openness and softness that is of your innermost.

As soon as there is a letting-go, as soon as the outermost of consciousness which has all the power and which is the you that you are accustomed to, begins to become honest and realize that what it is holding is not really needing to be held, it can begin to let go. Just a tiny little bit of movement, even just a tiny, seemingly invisible softening of the holding and gripping, brings about a response from the innermost of consciousness to participate with that softening and side with it. And it is like ointment.

What that does is draw the outermost of consciousness to give in more. The outermost of consciousness is being wooed by the innermost to continue, to just let go, to soften. And the more that openness and softness happens, the more there is space for the innermost to participate with a way of being that is presently happening in the outermost of consciousness. When there is an absolute, clean letting-go, it is only then that an absolute union of consciousness between the innermost and the outermost can occur. Now consciousness is actually living and functioning as one unified whole. You can go deep into the innermost and you can go far out to the outermost, and the way of being between the outermost and the innermost of consciousness will be the same.

III. INNERMOST - OUTERMOST

There is no separation. There is no different way of being between the one and the other.

For you, for the outermost of consciousness to let itself be warmly okay in realizing that it has been betraying the innermost, then a softness and an openness will happen. That is the outermost of consciousness being pierced in realizing something. In the midst of that piercing, hanging on does not work. There is a brokenness, a wonderful, nurturing, healing brokenness that happens in the outermost of consciousness. What it begins to realize is what it is doing, what it was being, and what that has been doing to the innermost.

That brokenness that occurs is a new flow of softness. It is newness flowing through something old. As soon as you are hard on yourself in any way at all in realizing that you have betrayed your own being, then that is just betraying it again. As soon as you are hard on yourself after realizing that being hard on yourself is betraying your being, then you are just doing the same thing once more. Your being does not have a problem with any of this, just as long as you let it go, just as long as you let yourself be as okay with having betrayed your own being, as your own being is okay with it.

Your own being does not hang onto the fact that you betrayed it. It does not function in resentment or bitterness. Your being is "letting-go-ness." It has no issue at all. The innermost never has any issue with what the outermost is inflicting on it. It will never hold onto anything, it will never hold against. And if you are holding something against yourself, then you are doing something that your innermost is not doing. Now you can warmly let it go in the only way that you know is true, being warmly okay that you have betrayed your own innermost, betrayed your own being.

Warmly being okay and warmly letting-go are things that are like perception – they'll come to me. Otherwise, I don't know how to be okay.

You can be warmly okay with not knowing how to be okay. Okayness is a function of being. The moment you take okayness and try to confine it by a mental construct or an emotional construct, then you are left with an idea, and you take that idea and you try to do that idea of okayness. It will not work. As soon as you identify okayness in your surface vehicles, then all you are identifying is a construct you have put together. It is only consciousness looking through the mind and the emotions, relating to something it has built that seems like okayness. And everything that it builds that seems like okayness, will never work. Okayness is the natural state of a true way of being. It is not something you can do, it is something you can *let* be.

When consciousness releases its hold inside of the surface vehicles, it begins to let go of identifying with them. If consciousness allows itself to rest from having to do, rest from striving and trying to be, then what remains in that rest is a function of being that is okayness. Resting from having to do is a healing of consciousness. What happens in that rest is nurture: consciousness itself being nurtured by what comes up from its innermost.

Consciousness is not nurtured by mental constructs or ideas. It is not nurtured by emotions. It is not nurtured by a physical state of wellness, nor by feelings of peace, love or joy. Consciousness is only truly nurtured when it finally lets go of ever needing to have peace, love or joy, lets go of trying to please the being, in its own innermost. Nurture happens when consciousness finally drops all of that, stops seeking, stops doing, stops striving and is content to just be, as is.

When consciousness is content to be, even if it perceives that it is a total screw-up, then what happens is a warm and unconditional contentment that it is now okay to forever be that screw-up without it ever needing to change. It is the okayness in being that kind of screw-up that allows the outermost to be just like the innermost. The innermost is not concerned if the outermost is screwed-up, just as long as the outermost is okay with it, as long as it is not trying to change it. The outermost cannot change anything. True change only comes from the innermost. The outermost can only let be whatever is. If the outermost is trying to change, it is trying to do something that it has no capacity to do.

I've heard you say "change comes from the innermost." Could you say more about that?

When you are creating your own reality – using a belief system and a moral structure, using information, ideas and ideals – then you as the outermost of consciousness are living out a reality which is not true. What is happening is that you as the outermost of consciousness are contorting and distorting yourself to be what you want to be. When you as outermost consciousness move into a state of contortion and distortion, you are wounding yourself, damaging yourself. You are making yourself be something that you are not. You are holding yourself in that state of distortion of outer consciousness and when you finally let go, completely let go to be okay, as is, that distortion stays. It does not immediately go. It does not go back to what it once was, because you have held it there long enough that the pattern of distortion holds itself. So as outermost consciousness you have actually wounded yourself.

It does not matter if that distortion never ever leaves and if it were to never heal, just as long as your way of being returns to one that is actually true while the distortion itself remains. Your innermost, the innermost of consciousness, has no problem with the distortion. To the innermost, to your true being, the presence of distortion does not matter. The loss of distortion does not matter either, as long as the outermost of consciousness returns to a way of being that is true. And then the outermost and the innermost can flow as one, through that distortion. What will move through that distortion is cleanness, a clean flow of consciousness. If the distortion were to never heal, never change, it truly would not matter.

But it just happens to be that the distortion does heal, does change. When the outermost of consciousness opens up and returns to a way of being that is true, that leaves it in a true state of stillness and rest, while the distortion remains. Now the innermost of consciousness has room to flow. It participates and it responds with the outermost and it moves all the way through. When that flow is moving through, that heals the distortion. The distortion will begin to match what comes from the innermost where there is no distortion, and it will follow.

When that clean flow of innermost consciousness is allowed to move through the outermost, the distortion heals and begins to unscramble. It begins to come alive once again and return to an original state of non-distortion. The innermost does not mind if there is outermost distortion. Any change in the outermost will happen by the innermost just simply flowing through it. But when the outermost dislikes the state that it is presently in and tries to change it or undistort, it has to distort even more, instead of just letting the healing take place on its own. And it only gets worse.

Until you become warmly and unconditionally accepting of what you have done, the damage cannot be corrected. You do not have to fix it. You do not have to change anything, just be okay, as is. That is enough. It is enough to please your entire innermost being. Your warm and unconditional acceptance of what you have done will allow the damage to heal without your effort. That simple okayness in the outermost of consciousness is so pleasing to the innermost, that the innermost cannot resist moving in response to and participating with it. Then love happens.

And love is something that the outermost cannot do. Peace is something that the outermost cannot do. The outermost cannot do anything but be wonderfully okay. All of the real doing comes right from the innermost and is expressed all the way through. It will look like the outermost is doing it. But when the outermost is honest, it knows it is not doing it. It is just being okay and seemingly doing what is happening, which is really a fruit of being that arises from the innermost. It does not originate from within the outermost. So then the outermost is just wonderfully giving way to the innermost, and the innermost is most wonderfully expressing itself through the outermost. That is consciousness living in a state of wholeness where there is no separation.

Then, consciousness begins to awaken to what the outermost is really for, to how the innermost moves through the outermost, and to how the outermost makes way for the innermost to move through it. Consciousness as a whole begins to actually realize how it lives, how it flows, and how it works, all in a way that is true and effortless. Consciousness actually begins to integrate itself.

Now consciousness is growing up. It is developing and expanding. It is not just knowing what it is and knowing what is true, it is actually learning how to do, in a way that is true. When consciousness is growing like that – when true consciousness is happening, when honesty of consciousness is happening – then reality happens. Then true life from the innermost all the way through the outermost, expressed in all of this life, happens. That is what we are here for.

I understood you to say that it doesn't matter what's going on in the mind, it doesn't matter if we grab despondently in the mind.

Real honesty of consciousness is different than a consciousness reaching into the mental vehicle, which is like a glove, and using that glove to try to grab something. Then it is really consciousness doing the grabbing, using the glove to do it and then blaming the glove for doing it.

Who or what is the glove?

The glove is the mental vehicle. And we blame that glove for everything. But for everything that glove is doing, it is consciousness or the hand within the glove that is really doing it, not the glove itself. The problem is not the glove, not the mind. It is only the dishonesty of consciousness within that vehicle of expression which can be blamed.

If it's not happening in the mind, then it's happening in consciousness.

There is one catch. When consciousness like a hand, reaches into the glove of the mind and begins to do in a way that is not true, then a vibrational pattern becomes established inside of the glove. It becomes reinforced every time consciousness, as the hand, uses the glove to try to get what it wants, and do in a way that it actually knows is not true. A vibrational pattern of thoughts becomes established in the mental vehicle. Then, when the hand as consciousness actually comes to rest, comes to a place of stillness where it is no longer doing to be and no longer using the mind to get it, then that vibrational pattern that was set up keeps happening.

So while consciousness is resting, resting from doing to be through the mind, circular patterns still continue. They are the same patterns that consciousness itself established in the mind, now playing on their own. The vibration continues. And what gives the energy that is being used for that vibration to continue is circumstance and the people around you. They provide energy to the old patterns in you, they make something matter about you that they actually, honestly know does not matter. They are using their own patterns; they are reaching up through their own emotional, intuitional, mental, volitional and physical vehicles, and they are giving energy to something concerning you as consciousness that is visible in your surface vehicles. That re-energizes the vibrational pattern that you set up in your surface vehicles. And even though you may be at rest as consciousness and in a place of actual okayness, your mind comes back into that same vibrational pattern that you set up.

Then you will have a mental experience of hanging on. You will have an emotional experience of hanging on, even though you as consciousness are not. It may be that you are in a place of rest and okayness as consciousness, but your thoughts and your feelings are being re-energized in a vibrational pattern of not-okayness. And if you use your thoughts and feelings to tell you what is happening, they will tell you you are hanging on. If you trust your thoughts and feelings, then you as consciousness will match those thoughts and feelings and you will

III. INNERMOST - OUTERMOST

hang on in the same way that that vibrational pattern of hanging on is doing. So now you will be one with that pattern.

As soon as you are warmly okay, as soon as you are in a way of rest in realizing that you are hanging on, then the pattern will continue to be what it is, but you will not be participating in the pattern. You as consciousness will be letting-go while a pattern of hanging on continues. It is just a repetitive pattern, playing itself out in the mind or the emotions. And what gives it energy is something outside of you. Someone else's not-okayness will give energy to not-okay patterns that you as consciousness set up. And that becomes your nearest opportunity to be okay, when they get touched.

When those patterns get touched and set off by something outside of you, while you are actually in a place of okayness, then you can warmly rest in openness and softness in the midst of the pattern, as is. It is not actually the fault of something that happens outside of you, because that something is only giving energy to a way that you have trained your mental vehicle to work. You have trained your own emotional vehicle to respond that way. You have mistrained as consciousness; you have mistrained and misused all of your surface vehicles. They continue to respond in the way that you taught them. And you get to be warmly okay with that, as is.

When the flow from your innermost is allowed to move and express itself through the outermost, then the moment that flow begins to touch old patterns that you set in place in your surface mental and emotional vehicles, those vehicles will begin to match that. They learn from that. And the old patterns will slowly begin to come undone and be replaced by a pattern that comes from the innermost: a pattern of truth, a way of being that is true. Over time, there will not only be a union between the innermost and the outermost of consciousness, but that union will actually begin to manifest right through to your surface vehicles. Your surface vehicles will also become just like the innermost and the outermost. Then there will be a manifested union of consciousness in form. That takes time. But the actual union of consciousness between the outermost and the innermost requires no time at all, just an absolute letting-go.

What I sense in myself in terms of letting-go, is that when you were in the UK there was in me a kind of naive openness.

Innocence.

And a letting-go of some sort. And that letting-go, since coming to Canada, has become like a struggle. I feel tightening, but it's okay.

It is awesomely okay. As soon as you realize how awesomely okay it is, then you will end up returning to the same space that was re-opened within you. In the UK you were re-acquainted with your innermost. And it was so lovely to you that you just dropped everything inside; you dropped everything that you were holding onto. You opened and softened within, and all that remained was this flow of being in love. You were re-acquainted with something that you always knew was true, and at the same time, you were so moved that it was really happening in you. There was just a beautiful, true response. There was an expression that came all the way from the innermost and moved right through the outermost. And there was a fulfillment of being, from its source all the way outward.

Then, you came to Canada, because there was a pull within. You knew that the way of being you were encountering in me was re-acquainting you as consciousness with what had always been within you. You had always known it was there, but everything you had tried in accessing it only made your problem worse. A bond of being happened in the UK between you as consciousness and what I am as consciousness. Because I re-acquainted you with what you always really were, it caused a pull.

But the outermost of consciousness is accustomed to trusting what it is thinking and feeling. So you came to Canada thinking that it would all continue. You came to Canada with feelings of hope. You came to

Canada with a construct coming together, a construct of expectation based on thoughts and feelings. So you were coming loaded. Then, when you arrived at where you expected a continuation of awakening to occur, you found yourself full of striving and trying. And you found yourself in pain, because you were so close to what had once been so far away. You were now so close to it and in the strangest way, you could not get it. Now to your thoughts and feelings, you were worse off than before.

Is it possible that I am actually worse off?

It will only seem that you are worse off. But it is only a thought and a feeling that is telling you that. It is only your old patterns that you are listening to. You are letting the old patterns tell you what is happening. While you are listening to those patterns, it seems there is something in them; it seems true, but it is different from what you actually know is true.

There is a complex knot that you have gotten into because of being awakened in the UK. What that awakening did is put all of your patterns into full gear because of the energy of awakening moving through them. There is nothing that moves patterns like awakening! So all those patterns worked themselves into a massive knot that is harder for you to untie than any knot that has ever been there before. And it is really okay, if it is allowed to be warmly and unconditionally okay. Then the flow that comes from the innermost will move through that massively complex knot. And it will all begin to unravel without any effort at all, without any doing to be.

The bit that I am not okay with is that it's as if I've lost the innocence that I had in the UK.

What is wrong with losing innocence? Was it yours anyway? The innocence came from your innermost. It expressed itself in the outermost. That gave you an experience of innocence. You realized that you were innocent, but it was not yours. It came from the innermost, it belonged to the innermost. It was the innermost expressing itself as innocence in the outermost. If that expression stops, it is not yours to grieve over once it is gone. It never belonged to you.

Then it's not lost.

Even if it is lost, it is not your problem. It is not for you to grieve and mourn over, because it never belonged to you. It was the innocence of your innermost. It is for you to be very, very tenderly okay in having seemingly lost the innocence that was realized in the UK, and that you were re-acquainted with. All those years you thought it was lost, it was never yours to be lost from. As soon as you were brought back to a way of being that is true, there was a return of innocence. But it was not yours. It was just that there was space in the outermost of consciousness for the innermost of consciousness to express what it really is, which is total innocence. You re-experienced innocence. If you can be awesomely okay in not experiencing that innocence again, then your innermost will have room again to express what it is, which is innocence.

Nothing that is true or real can ever be lost. You cannot damage reality, because your innermost is made of it. It is that. And the innermost is incorruptible. It cannot be defiled. It cannot be distorted. When the outermost tries to reach into the innermost with an agenda that is unclean, such as trying to get peace just to feel at peace, then at that moment, the outermost is functioning in a way of being that is unlike the innermost. When that incongruency occurs, the outermost has lost its capacity to be real. It will not find true peace. In that state it cannot even identify what the innermost really is.

With anything that the outermost thinks it is reaching into of the innermost, all it is really reaching into is an idea. And the most it can possibly do is use the surface vehicle of the will to add energy and try harder at this idea. It will create a construct which it calls the innermost, and it can try to reach into it by letting-go of everything and surrendering. But there is no cheating that works. Trickery does not work. You cannot get past that.

The only thing of the outermost that has access to the innermost is a way of being that is true. When the way of being of the outermost matches the way of being of the innermost, then the outermost without effort and without trying, without any constructs, has free access to dwell in the innermost. Then the innermost has free access to express itself through the outermost. And now there will be wholeness and completeness of consciousness. Now there will be true peace. It really is that easy. And it is as good as you always knew it to be; it is as beautiful as you always knew it to be.

It is baby-easy when you become re-acquainted with the way that is true. The moment you become re-acquainted with the way, you love it. And the moment you love it, there is a most warm disloyalty, an awesome disloyalty to every other way that you have ever tried. And you will take all of the ways that you have ever held together, all the other ways that you have been trying and forcing, putting together and holding together, and all of a sudden, you will just let them go. All of you, right from the core of your being, will be responding to the way of being that you always knew was so true, so easy, and so right.

There will be a warm disloyalty to a way of being that you thought or felt was true. That warm disloyalty looks like this: it easily lets go and it is no longer a way that is useful to you. What will be rekindled is a real love of truth, a love of a way of being that is true, an outermost love of something that originates from your own innermost being. When there is a love of that, then the same thing happens from your innermost toward the outermost. Love happens all the way from the innermost through the outermost. The flow is of the same. Now there is oneness of being. Now you are that being that you are serving. When your way of being is the same, you are that: you are a being.

For as long as there is some kind of holding on, some kind of exercise of control living and manifesting want and need, then you are not a being. Then you are a being acting out and pretending to be something that you are not. You are living an illusion. And that illusion aches.

I realized that attachment to the path is one of my biggest illusions because it gives me an identity.

And false hope: a false hope of continued awakening, a false hope of continued peace. When you no longer need awakening or peace, then the awakening continues. But then you are being in a state of true attachment. Then you are most wonderfully attached, supremely and only to what you actually know is true.

Now that is attachment of being, true addiction. It is when the outermost is completely sold out and addicted to just falling into the innermost; when the outermost is only giving itself up, giving itself away, free falling into the innermost. It is when the innermost can freely flow through the outermost in any way that it is moved to express itself. True addiction is when the outermost is addicted to serving and giving itself away to the innermost.

There is another true addiction that then occurs. It is the innermost addicted to expressing itself through the outermost. An awesome addiction of being is happening. You can try all the others, but none of them will fulfill like a true addiction of being!

Just let true in-loveness happen, not with what you think, not with what you feel, not with anything in your will where there is an in-loveness with want or need. But let there be an in-loveness with what you know. It does not matter how tiny that knowing of what is true seems to be. When you let in-loveness into that, the tiny little bit begins to expand and blossom and bloom.

And that tiny little bit will turn into all of you. It is only when there is in-loveness of consciousness with that tiny little bit that you actually know is true, that the outermost is being real. That is the only time that you are really being you.

III. INNERMOST - OUTERMOST

Is, for example, smelling a flower letting in in-loveness?

It is letting in in-loveness. The only difficulty is that it is happening through your surface vehicles. The mind knows what a flower is. It has a snapshot, an idea of what happens, and there is also an emotional response to what happens. Those patterns remain inside of the surface vehicles. But the mind also knows that if you smell a flower, something happens to you inside that neither the mind nor the emotions can comprehend. Every time you smell a flower, something deeper than the emotional response or the mental snapshot is touched. The mind and the emotional vehicles cannot reproduce what moves through them when the outermost is smelling the flower and there is that touch of the innermost that responds. So in-loveness with what you know does get touched when you smell a flower, but it is cloaked with surface body experience.

The smelling of that flower and what it does to you are not there for those awesome feelings of in-loveness. They are there to take you back to be the in-loveness that originates from your innermost. When you are smelling a flower, it is sending you back. It is reminding you of a way of being that is true, reminding you of something that does not originate from the you that you are accustomed to. It reminds you of a touch that does not come from the mind, the emotions, the will, the intuition or the body. There is an inner resonance that happens when you smell a flower, that tells you what is happening inside, what is taking place in you as consciousness while you smell a flower.

What is happening has nothing to do with anything in your whole life, the life of personal thoughts, emotions and intuitions that you have accustomed yourself to identifying with. It is not about that. It is really not about that. It is a response within from a way of being that is true, to something outside of you that is also in a way of being that is true. It is something that takes place all on its own, if you allow it. It is a response of truth, to truth. It has nothing to do with your self-constructed existence. So, in-loveness is there when you smell a flower, but it is reminding you and enlivening in you the part of you that actually recognizes that there is something real, when you smell a flower. Reality recognizes reality. It is reality within you, recognizing and responding to reality outside of you.

That letting in in-loveness could be the same whether I'm smelling a flower or I'm smelling fumes.

That is true. But then that in-loveness is much finer. When you are smelling fumes, there is nothing that is appealing to your surface vehicles. Your physical body does not like it. When your physical body does not like it, that produces a feeling in your emotional body or vehicle that is not very pleasant. It produces a thought in the mental vehicle as it is capturing everything happening, that puts an entire construct together and calls it: "Fumes being smelled are not nice, I don't like it, stay away from it." And all of that structure is okay as long as it is left to be shallow, left as an outermost perception that has nothing to do with what you are knowing deeper within, beneath all the sensory experience in your surface vehicles.

What is most often missed is that while all of this is happening, the in-loveness can still be there. The in-loveness is then much, much finer, because it is now in the midst of something that does not feel good and is not okay, physically. Then the fineness of the in-loveness is a knowing that it is actually okay, even though it does not feel okay. The smelling of fumes in the outermost of consciousness through sensory experience, cannot touch or take away or damage okayness within, unless you choose to let it.

As you begin to realize this in the midst of smelling the fumes that make you uncomfortable and physically not okay, what happens is a blossoming of okayness. There is the knowing that your okayness is not limited when being physically affected by fumes. This is a blossoming of reality or in-loveness in the midst of physical not-okayness. That kind of in-loveness is much finer, whereas the in-loveness that happens when you smell a flower is much coarser, much easier; you can't help it.

The coarser, easier kind is also addictive in terms of a feeling. What easily happens is that when you are not feeling okay and you see a flower, you go to smell it not for you to return to a way of being that is true, but to smell that flower and look at it for a feel-good. The patterns are all there in your mind, your emotions and your senses, and you remember what happens when you smell a flower, what it does to you inside.

We easily use something that is just like our innermost, for a feel-good. Then we get really smart and we go for walks in nature. And if there is a dishonesty of consciousness, then while we are walking in nature we suck from nature. We take, only for a feel-good. There is no oneness in that walk. There is just a thievery, there is just a taking. It is like saying: "I'll steal from nature its energy to get the joy and the peace and the love that I want." We do the same thing when we hold a cat, when we pet a dog.

When we hug?

Yes. And that does not mean not to go for walks anymore and not to pet dogs and hold cats and hug. It is just about letting honesty in. When honesty is let in, letting-go becomes increasingly more and more irresistible. There will be more of a draw, an expression to pet a dog, to hold a cat, to walk in nature. But it will no longer be to get. The expression will simply happen, because while you are walking in nature there will be such an incredible movement from your innermost all the way out; an expression of oneness with the very thing that you are walking in the midst of. This is so different from the way you have accustomed yourself to walking in nature. Everything changes.

Let in in-loveness, not with a thought or a feeling or an ideal, but in-loveness with what you know, in-loveness with a way of being, even if it is just a touch.

That in-loveness is not at all dependent on any outside stimuli?

It is dependent only on honesty. Then, when there happens to be an outside stimulus of being that directly connects with your innermost being, drawing up within you as consciousness an honesty or exposing a dishonesty, then that outside influence of honesty is actually displacing dishonesty in you. The in-loveness with what you know within begins to equally extend itself toward that influence of truth outside of you. Then, there is a response of in-loveness to something outside of you that is just like what is of your own innermost consciousness.

When you are allowing the in-loveness within you to respond to something outside of you that is enlivening or awakening your in-loveness, that takes you through to your innermost to be able to recognize it. Then, the more you respond to your innermost, the stronger the response will be to that outside source that is validating or enlivening your innermost. The more you respond to that outside source, the more your own innermost will open up and expand because your innermost is where the response is coming from. So then a bond of being will be taking place: a bond between you and your innermost of consciousness and at the same time, a bond between you as true consciousness and the outside source of the same truth, to which you are responding.

If it happens for me, it has to happen in the stillness, and I have the concept that I need stillness because I am not fine to let in-loveness just happen.

When you are actually still, not in your mind or your emotions, but within you as consciousness, then you will find that you are in love with that.

In love with what?

In love with what you know: with a true way of being, with openness and softness of heart, with stillness and with rest.

III. INNERMOST - OUTERMOST

When you say "stillness of consciousness" are you meaning honesty?

When consciousness becomes honest, it becomes still. As soon as consciousness becomes dishonest, it gets busy, and it starts doing what it does not need to do, starts trying what it does not need to try. It even tries ways of being that it actually knows do not work. When there is a dishonesty of consciousness, there is self-delusion happening. Consciousness ends up insisting on something that it knows is not true and that does not work. It insists that it has to work because it thinks that it just might, if it changes it this way or tries it that way. And that never works. But dishonesty will never cease trying.

When there is honesty of consciousness, it is the end of all trying. It is the end of all doing to be. Honesty of consciousness results in a true love of stillness and rest, for the true sake of stillness and rest.

CHAPTER 4

The Tiny Little Bit

Now you get to use all of your resources
to accommodate that
tiny little bit.

Now you know
your purpose in life.

Now you can
live and think and feel
and do and try and be,

and it is finally
all of that,
for one:
the right One.

All of that
in service
to that tiny little bit

IV. THE TINY LITTLE BIT

Questioner: In Boulder you talked about passion, and I wondered if you could talk about what role passion has with truth?

John: Passion is your capacity to let in life, your capacity to absorb life. The kind of passion that we are accustomed to is very narrow and highly conditional. To truly absorb life, without hesitation, restriction or condition of any kind, is to allow, from a true way of being, everything that is present in the moment to have complete access inside. To be that passionate in life you have to be home.

What we commonly relate to in terms of passion is not too little and not too much, if personal life experience is our frame of reference. In an attempt to cope with life we use passion. We just learn how to control it. We learn how much to let in and how far to let it go. It is only when you are home, residing in a true inner way of being of openness and softness and rest, that true passion can be unlocked. When you are not home, you will temper or condition your passion. Then you will have conditioned and tempered your capacity to let in everything of life.

So when you're home that passion is constant, it doesn't waver?

When you are home passion can move with freedom. That kind of passion can in one moment fill everything, and in the next moment be completely empty and you will have lost nothing. You are simply remaining in a true, inner way of being that fully allows the presence of passion and equally allows its absence, whichever presents itself at any given time.

When you are not home and there is a tempered passion, then whatever you are passionate about becomes something you are afraid to lose. If the passion happens to be there one moment and you invest yourself in the passion, you are aware that you will be left empty if something should take it away. So when you are not home, everything matters. You cannot afford to be truly passionate, since true passion could mean going way out on a limb without a thought of something cutting it, and without a thought of losing the something you have so carefully invested so much passion in.

When you are home and that limb does happen to get cut, it does not matter to you. You can afford to go way out on any limb that you know is true to go out on, without any thought of self-preservation. You can afford to gain or lose anything you have acquired and you can afford to gain or lose any passion that has been invested, since none of it was for you. It was never about you. You were simply remaining passionately present: home in a way of being that you knew to be true, allowing passion to completely fill you or completely leave you. Passion is your capacity to be passionately present, without condition, simply, in a way of being that is true.

So you're saying when you are home, passion might come in and fill something and then be gone?

With true passion it is like a little child being totally engrossed in something. Everything it is and everything it has is being poured into one focus. It would look as though to disturb that child in the midst of that focus would mean trouble. That little child is home in the midst of passion, right in the midst of what it is that is so engrossing. But you could easily pick that child up and he or she would turn to you and respond to you instead. That child will have lost nothing.

When a child or an adult is not home and is totally engrossed in something, then whatever might pick them up or distract them from their focus in a way that is beyond their control, means trouble. For them, it is like an investment has been lost. With true passion, when you are home, you are passionately present. Everything could be taken away from you and you will have always lost nothing. That is being truly alive.

You refer to consciousness within us or truth within us as a "tiny little bit." Whenever I hear that, I have a feeling of it being under-valued in some way. I feel like it's worthier to refer to it as being larger than a tiny little bit.

IV. THE TINY LITTLE BIT

My tiny little bit is immeasurably smaller than yours.

You're saying that being little is not a negative reference here if it's smaller within you; it's not undervaluing?

The smaller the little bit you can go to, the deeper you are within consciousness or reality, the closer you are to the absolute source. In all of your opening and softening and diminishing and dissolving and remaining in the tiny little bit that you know is true, could you let the dissolve and the disintegration go straight through, straight inside of and through that little bit and never stop? Then that little bit you have gone so deeply inside of will become, to you, like a whole universe.

Within that whole universe which was once, to you, just a tiny little bit, will you open and soften and diminish and dissolve and rest in the fineness of a new, ever tinier little bit that you now know is true, from a now much finer way of being? Then, with each opening and softening and diminishing and disintegrating, you will be dropping deeper and deeper into reality. Truth or reality will become deeper and more and more expansive, the more you, as consciousness, merge with it and realize it.

The more you allow only the tiniest little bit that you know is true to be your sufficiency, the greater your realization of reality and truth will become. And the you that you were accustomed to will become less and less and less and less. It is going from form back to formlessness. And it is only within the tiniest little bit, or within the least that you find the most. It is fineness within the most tender of what you know to be true, that unveils the depth of reality or truth.

I want to hear you talk about sex. What is truth within that experience?

The very simplest is that it is not for you – the you that you think or feel you are, the you that you are accustomed to.

So it doesn't belong to me, it just exists as a flow? What is it for then?

It is something that belongs to truth, belongs to your innermost consciousness. It is an avenue of expression through which your innermost can most wonderfully move. Sexuality is for that tiny little bit that you know is true, within you. It does not belong to the rest of you. You may take it and use it, but it is not yours. The more of a tight hold you have on anything to do with sex, the more of an ache there will be inside. The more wonderfully there is a complete and absolute letting-go of any self-oriented wanting or using of sexuality for yourself, the more the tiny little bit will have an arena to be in and express itself. Sexuality is something profoundly other than how people are generally accustomed to understanding and using it.

Sex of a self-oriented nature is another one of the things that does not work. It becomes something to want and to need and it just leaves people identifying with wanting and needing. People use it to get something and that is where it fails. It is only meant for expression, not for getting anything. It is not for the expression of you, the you that you are accustomed to. It is for the expression of that tiny little bit that you know is true, that comes from your innermost. Sexuality belongs to that.

When that tiny little bit of reality is expressing itself through sexuality, that tiny little bit expands into that arena, and it becomes huge. It reveals itself. But the moment you touch it – that is, use it in any way for the you that you are accustomed to, because you like it for that you – then the tiny little bit recedes from expression. It goes right back down to a tiny little bit, deep within your innermost. It will leave you to have that space and do anything with it you want. And there will never be a fulfillment of being, because you do not belong there. Your being does. None of this really, really works unless you are home. So sex is only for those who are home.

So if you like sexuality and you're not home what happens?

IV. THE TINY LITTLE BIT

Liking sexuality is fine. But when you are touching it – that is, using it for the you that you are accustomed to, because you like it – then the tiny little bit that you know is true will let you have what you want. That tiny little bit of reality, of what you know is true, will recede. There is nothing that works until you are home. Nothing really, really works until you are home – not relationships, not sexuality, not passion – nothing works.

If there is pain or if there are negative emotions that come up, are they a barrier to really being what you are, to really being?

Pain is a window or a doorway to being what you really are. But it has its own threshold. You cannot really experience and move through pain unless there is a warm okayness, an allowing of innermost rest regardless of outer emotions or pain. Then, when you are in that true way of being, you can truly move through pain. And every time there is some kind of pain, then for you it will be another doorway or window, deeper into that little bit of what you know is real. That will result in endless new ways of knowing and being through depths of your own innermost consciousness. Pressure of every kind creates a window for realizing the depths of your innermost being.

What we tend to do is deal with those windows in a way that is not clean, not honest. We call them something bad and then there is an avoidance. We go away from them, instead of going into them and letting in whatever we are encountering. We avoid touching, in a true way, what is really happening to us inside.

What would happen if you were to move into a space of total vulnerability? What if from that openness, that softness, that space of total vulnerability, pain were allowed in, allowed to go anywhere inside of you and do anything to you? If you had any need of coping you would lose the vulnerability, lose that window of realization.

If there is a warm letting-go of needing to cope, then pain moving through a space of total vulnerability would crack you wide open. It would crack you open as consciousness. And things would happen inside of you as consciousness that you will have never experienced before. As long as there is no need to cope, you as consciousness would do just fine. You would begin to experience in new depths and new ways what you really, really are.

When pain cuts inside of you as consciousness and you let it in, then everywhere it cuts and everything that the pain touches becomes realized as consciousness. Pain is like an instrument of awakening; pain can get into places inside of you that you have never been before.

But if there is any need to cope, if there is any need to relate to the familiar, then you will never let that pain go there. You will direct the pain to go into a part of you that you are familiar with. You will use the pain on yourself, the you that you think and feel you are, the you that you are accustomed to. You will take that pain and you will turn it into self-abuse. You will use it to be hard on yourself, because that way it stays in an arena that you are already familiar with.

For that pain to be allowed to go into an unfamiliar arena, into the depths of you as consciousness that you have not yet awakened to or realized, then you would discover that you do not understand you. You do not understand what you are. You do not understand why you are here. And as the pain is moving into unknown and unrealized places in you as consciousness, you would seemingly lose everything. All that is presently familiar to you could not describe to you what is happening.

It is only when you are home that you can actually let pain in. And you can let it in anywhere inside of you and completely leave your hands off. From the space of total vulnerability you can let pain go anywhere inside, and you can let it freely move. It will crack you open as consciousness, and it will leave you raw in a way that you have never been raw before: gently lost in rawness, without any understanding of what is going on.

You said you have to be totally willing to die to allow that to happen. Is that

IV. THE TINY LITTLE BIT

true?

Warmly be open to allow the dying of your self-created mental and emotional constructs and attachments – the dying of the untrue you. This only happens with those who are returning home. To the degree that you are not home, you will resist dying. And you will hold onto living. But that is not real living, it is holding onto a conditional kind of living. It is avoiding real living, because that would make you vulnerable, create too much wide open space inside, too much flow of a reality that you do not understand with your mind and do not feel familiar with. In conditional living there is constant striving to keep the flow in areas that are presently familiar. So, inasmuch as you are not home, you cannot let in brand new life, brand new flow. That would be to you like letting in something completely unknown.

To let in the unknown is to be consumed by something that you cannot even comprehend. You would continually lose the understanding and feeling of home that you are familiar with, so that you could merge with something unfamiliar, something new. It is only when you are deepening as consciousness in home that you can turn into something that you have never been before. It is only when you are home that you can be something completely new.

For you as consciousness to open up, and for the outermost of consciousness to gain access into an aspect of the innermost where it has never been before, the outermost will lose itself. It will turn into what it is accessing. It will lose all of its familiarity; it will cost you everything. You will lose what you are in terms of what you are familiar with.

I might as well go for it. How do I begin?

Then you can let go of holding inside everything that you are presently familiar with, everything that you have ever learned through any kind of experience or any kind of awareness, everything that you have taken in and stored up inside. Let it go. All that you lose is what is presently familiar to you. All you lose is all of you. That you that you are accustomed to is only the identification with the familiar. You hold onto it inside and illegitimately call it you.

Turning that familiarity into an internal structure, you make your way around with the use of it. But you will have comprehension only of what you have already internalized. You might study that familiarity, study the you that you think you are. But the more you study it, the more complex your structure will become and the more you will turn into a you that is, in reality, not you at all.

If you let go of all of what you presently think and feel you are – your belief structure, your moral structure and let go inside of everything that you have ever learned or ever acquired inside – then what will remain is something new. And the first touch of newness, the tiny little bit that comes up and replaces the familiar, is worth more than everything that you let go of. That first tiny little bit of newness that replaces the familiar, that is the real you. The real you is that little bit of newness that constantly moves into your awareness without you ever touching it. It moves in, straight through and out. It is a continual flow of newness such that all you are is that. You are newness. Anything that appears as being familiar is just simply okay, but it will never be you again. What happens is that consciousness begins to realize itself. You will actually find out what you as consciousness really are.

For any part of you as consciousness that identifies with control or coping or familiarity, this is the epitome of absolute terror. It is flying straight into something that is absolutely new; a space that you have not a clue about. Flying into outer space would not be flying into newness, because you already have familiarity with that. You can look at it from here. There may be something new about it, but there would still be a frame of reference you could comprehend. You would still be moving through something that your mind could understand. When real awakening happens, you would be flying through absolute newness with no familiar frame of reference at all.

IV. THE TINY LITTLE BIT

Sounds like fun.

Only if you are home. Only if you are already existing as consciousness in a true way of being. If you are not home, that is not fun. If you are not home and something like that could be forced on you – such as going into newness whether you liked it or not – you would lose your mind, you would strain your surface vehicles. What your surface vehicles would be manifesting is how much it is true that you, in your present state of consciousness or way of being, cannot handle this. If you as consciousness could not handle it, then your surface vehicles would not be able to handle it either.

In reality, there is nothing more fulfilling than real awakening happening. But it is only fulfilling if you are home. If you are not home, then just one touch of it and inside, all of you will just shrink and jump back with everything that you are.

Being here is beyond anything that I could ever imagine. I am so grateful for your being and for my littlest bit that I feel I have been clueless about on a certain level. On another level it's gotten me here.

It feels like I've consolidated my whole life and my patterns. I've consolidated my not-okayness and my running from my not-okayness, my buying into the lie of my separation, my not connecting with my littlest bit. I feel like I have nothing to lose by letting all that go, although I know it's not going to be a picnic – far from it. But there is nothing else to do.

That is true.

Whenever you gave what seemed to be instructions about being open or soft, I was turning them into a discipline, the "John discipline." I realized that you're trying to present a way for people to hear through your words and through your energy, how to be and how to open to that being. It's not a discipline but it sounds like one, just because I haven't been in that state of being.

That is true.

I've never trusted anybody in my life. I haven't trusted the world, I haven't trusted myself and yet I have total trust in you. I can't believe that I can go home, that it's possible to go home, and that you're truth and we're truth. How is this happening?

I live absolutely and unconditionally surrendered to ever deepening depths of home, surrendered to innermost consciousness, reality, truth. I exist in that way of being regardless of any personal cost. I exist only to serve truth and I function as that truth. My way of being is what is awakening a true way of being in you.

What do I need to do to get beyond my very strong mental body and all of my distrust? How can I continue to open and receive? What do I need to know from you that would serve truth, my littlest bit, to the utmost?

Continue with what is already happening in you by living and trusting my way of being more than you; by living, loving what I am as a way of being, more than the you that you are familiar with.

Is it that simple? One of the greatest hindrances that I see is that when I feel this littlest bit, I feel like my ego, the not-okayness, is trying to feel better or be propped up by what it perceives the being is doing.

It is not even worth focusing on. Instead of letting-go of that focus on what your being is doing, what does the little bit inside that you know is true, look at? It does not look at your ego, your patterns, your life or your past. It does not look at your feelings or any idea inside of you. That little bit does not even see you. But that little bit is wide-eyed toward what I am, wide-eyed toward a way of being that it recognizes as true. That, it responds to.

IV. THE TINY LITTLE BIT

But that just seems to happen automatically. I heard a tape of you today, and it occurred to me that just to listen with openness, without even trying to grasp the words, is enough.

If you were to sit in this room and not understand the English language, you would get it. You would be listening to every word that I would be speaking, but you would not be listening with the mind. Regardless of the you that you are accustomed to, your being would be coming right through and listening in a way that only it knows. And while your being is listening, it would be totally bypassing all of the you that you have ever been familiar with.

Your being knows that what I am is a way of being like itself. Your being does not know what you are. So your being listens to what I am; it never listens to the old you. If it had listened to you, then what you would have done is woo your being to come up. As soon as it was within grasp, you would have reached out and stolen everything that it is, used it to cope and to control and to be happy. You would have used it for pain relief and it knows that. Your being does not respond to you. It does respond to what I am, because what I am is of the same reality as that tiny little bit in you. When you come into the space of being that I am, your being responds and it is naturally moved to flow outward.

I shouldn't hold onto this space of being. I feel like that's going to be my hardest attachment to let go of it.

It is not about holding onto that space of being, because you do not need anything. You do not need to be home. Home is wonderfully none of your business. Home is something that belongs to that tiny little bit in you. For you to have recognition of what I am, then it is not the you that you are accustomed to who is doing the recognizing. It is that tiny little bit inside of you that is coming up and watching what I am, and knowing what I am. You know what I am because it is already in you. When you are loving what I am – trusting what I am, valuing what I am as a real way of being more than the you you are accustomed to – then you are at that moment in the space of that tiny little bit, that same true way of being without even trying.

When I tried it didn't work.

Everything that you tried did not work. But everything that the tiny little bit in you responds to, you can respond to with all of your space by giving that up for the tiny little bit and whatever it is responding to. It gets to have the space that you are accustomed to living in.

All I want to do is to be true to the tiniest little bit. How do I do that?

Then give it everything. Let it decide what is real, instead of you. Let it decide what has value, instead of you deciding through what you think and feel. Give up your whole existence just to accommodate that tiny little bit. Use everything that you are, to give to that tiny little bit inside that you know is true.

I'll do that gladly. A little fear comes up but not a lot, just because I don't know what I am in for.

The tiny little bit knows what it is in for. That is all that it sees.

The tiny little bit can take me home?

Home is you letting that tiny little bit have you. Home is when that tiny little bit is allowed to control you, have you, master you, move you, do anything within you that it is wonderfully moved to do. And all you will ever do is give. And you will never want anything back. You will live as a beloved servant to that tiny little bit. You will exist only and most wonderfully to give way to it.

IV. THE TINY LITTLE BIT

Will you help guide me on this journey?

I am already that space that it loves.

Would it be best to move here, to Edmonton?

What does it move toward most? To be here or to be there? If you know that, then respond to the inclination of the tiny little bit that you know is true. Then you will piece together this entire existence in form, just so that the formless tiny little bit has a way of getting to where it responds and to where it is moved to be. You can use all of everything that you have acquired, everything that you ever learned, everything that you are presently familiar with, to put something together in this existence, so that the tiny little bit can be where it is inclined to be. Then you will finally be using all of your resources for it, instead of for you.

You are accustomed to using your resources to get happiness, to acquire pain relief. Now you get to use all of your resources to make possible for that tiny little bit to have whatever it would like. Now you know your purpose in life. You can work and live and think and feel and do and try and be. And it is finally all of that for one, the right one, for that tiny little bit. Now your career has a purpose. It can be used for that tiny little bit. Now your mind has value. You can execute short term and long term goals, just so that the tiny little bit can have the life that it wants. All of your goals, all of your capacity to work with goals, will now be in service to that tiny little bit.

How do I stay grounded throughout all of this?

In terms of what you are accustomed to, your way of becoming grounded is being in familiar territory inside, which has nothing to do with that tiny little bit. You do not need to be grounded. For you to be wonderfully okay without having any sense at all of being grounded, that is true groundedness. The sense of groundedness that you are accustomed to is mental, emotional, intuitional, volitional and physical, but it has no groundedness of being. So it misses; it's not it.

You were talking a lot about loving that tiny little bit, but I couldn't really picture myself loving – doing a loving. And then you were talking about how loving is a fruit of being; it's not something that you do, it's a being kind of thing. Maybe you could weave those two together for me in a way that somehow makes more sense to me.

As soon as you as consciousness give everything that you are to what I am as a true way of being, then there is this response that comes back, I give everything that I am to you. All of what I am, which is of the same as the little bit that you are, now has a direct relationship of being. And that is all that truly remains. Now that tiny little bit lives inside of what it can see outside of itself, which is just the same as itself only much, much deeper. And then that tiny little bit automatically begins to match that depth, because it sees and it knows, and it responds.

In a moment like this I feel there is really nothing for me to do but what I'm doing by being here. And at other times my mind gets pretty active, especially when I hear you talking to other people and all the processes that people are going through in order to be here and I feel, maybe I'm not doing enough; maybe I have to put some effort into it and understand more, give up more, suffer more.

The way that it works is by true osmosis. And the you that you are accustomed to has the capacity to get in the way of that true osmosis, because it knows what is happening. It realizes the implications, so it may get in the way and try to filter out that osmosis. Or, when it lets honesty in, the you that you are familiar with may recognize that the osmosis is of more value than itself. Then, as it begins to open up and become honest, it will see and it will recognize. The you that you are accustomed to will just simply step aside and be present in a way that it knows is true.

IV. THE TINY LITTLE BIT

The me that I am used to will do that, just get out of the way, nicely and graciously?

Yes. When it gets honest it becomes gracious, favouring that little bit in you that is responding to the same way of being that I am. All I represent to you is a way of being, a way of being that you know is true, a way of being that you love, a way of being that you truly respond to right from your innermost.

I feel gratitude for whatever it was that led me to you. I know you say that prayers don't work, but maybe it's just coincidence.

What works is honesty, the smallest little particle of honesty. That will always lead you inasmuch as you will allow, into depths of a way of being that are within your innermost of consciousness. Even if you were almost completely hardened in dishonesty, if all that remained was just one little particle of honesty in you as consciousness, then it would be that little particle of honesty that would recognize instantly what a true space is.

That one little particle of honesty would vibrate in a way that it never vibrated before. It would just hum. That tiny little particle would go into song, and the sweetness of that song would be so irresistible that the weaker part of dishonesty in you as consciousness would get pulled in and become part of the song. A momentum would begin until a total shift in consciousness would take place. Prayers do not work. Absolute and unconditional honesty toward the tiniest little bit that you know is true, does.

CHAPTER 5

Enlightenment Through Endarkenment

While there is
dryness,
emptiness,
darkness,
lifelessness,
hopelessness,
blindness,
you can
let that state
be warmly
and unconditionally
okay,
forever.

Total rest inside;
everything as is.
Complete.
Tender.
Real.

It is not about
getting the light.
Awakening is
tender okayness
in light or dark.
Sweetness or
piercing,
you could not choose,
even if there were
choice.
You could only let be
what really is,
whatever really is,
forever.

V. ENLIGHTENMENT THROUGH ENDARKENMENT

Questioner: You were talking about the truth and even the smallest lie, how the being will step aside and allow that. Well I have a lot of lies, and sometimes I feel that I get lost in some of them. I remember reading Carlos Castaneda, the Don Juan book. He is on the edge of a cliff with his so called master and they are holding hands, and the last words in this particular book are that they jump together. So is that possible? Can I take your hand right now and just jump? I Is there an edge that we can go to? Can we do it? I don't want to feel pain, I don't want to feel hurt, I don't want to feel trapped.

John: There is something wrong with that.

With being trapped?

There is nothing wrong with being trapped.

But I find something wrong with that. I don't like the experience.

Being trapped is really okay. Wanting to not feel trapped, that is not okay.

I don't want it. It's like Krishnamurti said: "You jump out of the house when you see it's on fire, you don't sit in a house that is on fire."

Yes, you do. An outside house that is on fire, you run out of. If your house inside is on fire, you be in it. It is just acceptance of what truly is. There is no need to change your space inside. What is wrong with there being a fire inside, burning up your inside house when you are in it?

You're going to get burned alive, or you're going to defend your self against the fire.

Then you get to be warmly okay with dying in your inside house.

So I just lie down?

Warmly. Anything less than that, and you will still be wishing that you were in a different space. The only kind of acceptance that works is warm acceptance.

Is there a difference between compliance and just saying: "What the hell, I am not going to get out of here, so I might as well just lie down and turn on the TV?"

That is cold acceptance.

So just lie down, turn on the TV and ...

That is just fatalism. That is non-acceptance not being able to get its own way. If you are not light, you cannot have any light, you can have darkness. If you can be warmly okay in darkness, then that is where light comes from. Light does not come out of a place of not-okayness. Light only comes out of a place that is profoundly accepting. The more unconditionally okay you can be in the dark, the more light there will be. The more light that you want or need, the darker it will become inside in a very not-okay way.

While there is dryness, emptiness, darkness, lifelessness, hopelessness or blindness, you can let that state be warmly and unconditionally okay, forever. You can come to total rest inside, letting-go of this state ever needing to change, warmly letting-go of ever needing to alter or fix it. No one little part in it needs to change. Everything can stay as is, and what you can do is just simply be okay in it, really okay in it. Be so okay that if someone with great power were to ask: "Is there anything inside that you would like changed?" that you would not know how to answer. That kind of okayness would be so complete, so whole, so tender inside, so real, so full of life, so kind and healing inside, that there would be nothing that you could honestly think of inside that if it changed, would

V. ENLIGHTENMENT THROUGH ENDARKENMENT

make that okayness better. You would not know how to answer. And you would be awakened to what is real. And yet nothing within the space that you were in would have changed. Only you would be different in that space.

True awakening is when, if you were to come to a fork in the road, and one way would be awesome bliss, total bliss, and the other fork would be total pain and suffering inside, the kind that would completely tear you apart, that you would not know which way to go. You would not have a preference. What you would do at the head of that fork, is go by the tiniest, tiniest little indicator that comes from your being. If there were some slight, tiny little preference of being, a tiny little pull one way or another, that would determine which way you would go. And the fact that one way is bliss and the other way is suffering would not make any difference to you at all. That is freedom.

If you are in bliss and you are happy about that, glad that it is so, then you will suffer more. Bliss is not worth anything unless you can be there without attachment, without preference. And the suffering also does not mean anything unless you can be in it without attachment and without preference. When you become awakened, and especially when you later become enlightened, you will freely be inside of pains that you cannot possibly conceive of now. So if pain is not okay now, you really do not want awakening or enlightenment.

Awakening is only for the unconditionally okay. If you let yourself be unconditionally okay, no matter what kind of not-okayness you are in, then awakening will happen. And if you remain in that kind of clean, clear, honest, true space of being – okay under every imaginable or unimaginable pressure – then enlightenment will begin to happen. Enlightenment only happens inside of great darkness where there is profound okayness. It is not about getting the light, it is about tender okayness in the dark.

If you were to hold my hand and jump off the edge, I would be jumping into depths and spaces and abysses of not-okayness that you presently do not know about. What would be jumping in would be okayness, and it would not stop itself from going into any depth. I would not be jumping into an okay kind of place. But I would be being okay jumping into anything that I knew was true to jump into, without hesitation.

For you to be closer to me, for you to be closer to what I am as a true way of innermost being, then you would become intimately acquainted with okayness inside of many different dimensions and depths of not-okayness. You would become acquainted with a depth of okayness inside of such incredible not-okayness, that all that would come out of you would be brilliant light – the brilliant light of real okayness. And that light of okayness would shine inside of every kind of not-okayness. Only light-bearers can truly go into dark places.

If you were to reach full awakening and then move into enlightenment, and if you met someone who was dark inside – dry, brittle, sick inside, extremely not okay and totally hopeless, not able to see anything inside – then would you, without any hesitation, be willing to just simply for good, trade places? Or would you hesitate and rather somehow preserve at least what you are in, give something away so long as you get to keep what you presently have? True compassion is when there is no hesitation in just simply trading places and doing it in such a way that it is not anything important. It is not even a sacrifice. It is just simply okay to do so. That is what love is like.

If you were to follow me, all I would teach you and show you is how to be compassionate. You would learn, first toward yourself, and you would learn with the simplicity of okayness. You would learn how to lay your head down inside, warmly, in the midst of anything. You would learn how to rest, how to warmly rest inside in the midst of any kind of pressure, any kind of not-okayness. You would learn to let tender acceptance have freedom to go anywhere inside of you, and you would always move in agreement. You would always acquiesce. You would never, under any kind of pressure, kick or fuss. You would never murmur inside. You would never complain inside. The only response that you would ever have in the midst of any kind of internal not-okayness would be a simple, tender okayness.

Then I would be able to teach you more. Then I could take you to deeper places in which the first teaching would have to be completely settled inside, rooted and immovable so that nothing could pull you out of it. You would be that surrendered to a way of being that is just complete okayness in everything, as is. Once that is set, then there are many places that we could go. If that is not set, then this is the first place for you to go. This is the first way for you to give in inside until this true way of being totally and completely replaces all other ways of being that you have always known were never really good enough.

That is where I come from and that is the only place I can take you: to completely open up inside, to be in the very, very beginning of true development, true movement, true flow. This is not a place to arrive at, this is a space that can open up inside of you. Then you would be in the space of beginnings.

For such a space to open up, that is where it will all start. That is where you will begin to learn how to move about as a being, a kind of movement in which there is no ego. You will learn to move about as a being, to do as a being and to do beingness; how to transmit or impart beingness without touching someone's personality, without touching their ego, their not-okayness. You will learn how to do that in such a way that only their okayness, deep, deep inside, far underneath gets touched. It will get pulled right to the surface in such a way that only a tender, irresistible response to give into that will occur. And that will cause that person to leave behind the perceived largeness of everything that on the inside, that person allowed to push him or her around, everything that made that person's life so miserable.

You will learn to give no energy to that, to respond only to the tiny little bit being touched within that person, until that begins to grow like a little sprout until a tree of life begins to emerge within them. It is learning how to be just awesomely at home in any kind of darkness. Enlightenment is a fruit of becoming warmly endarkened. You can only bring light to the kind of dark places that you can genuinely be in, without light.

I would be taking you home right through the middle of the very worst. Then you would find out how close home has always been, even in the midst of the worst. Those are the depths that I come out of to take people back into, but in a way that is so wonderfully okay. That is the good news I have.

Once you have let this kind of energy in, you can never erase its imprint. It is the only kind of energy that your being forever loves. It is the only kind of energy where the ego actually knows it does not have a chance. You will realize that as deeply as you let its sweetness in is how deeply you will also be pierced. Letting in the sweetness is the giving of permission to let yourself taste what is real. That changes everything, effortlessly. A depth of okayness, really profound okayness will open up with the sweetness. And that okayness, that true innermost rest, is what will show you how to be okay in the midst of any kind of piercing. It is just as easy to be okay in sweetness as in piercing. Only one feels good and the other does not.

You've been dishing "okayness" out already, but could you please dish out some more, and does it go to everyone or can I have some now?

You do not need any. No one needs any okayness. You can let yourself be unconditionally okay with never, ever being okay again. That is okayness. You are equating okayness with a feeling and okayness is not a feeling and it is not a thought. It is the way of inner honesty and surrender. It is the way of being that is simply true.

I heard what you said to that man over there, and that sounded pretty scary.

In talking with him, I was also provoking honesty in you.

In me? I believed it was necessary to have a dialogue with you.

V. ENLIGHTENMENT THROUGH ENDARKENMENT

On the inside, you have need of nothing. You no longer need to try to get anything at all. You can love that someone is actually living in it. That is enough. You can cherish that it is actually happening somewhere. And that is enough. That would be a love of truth in you, because it is only truth in you that can see it outside of you. It is only your honesty within that allows you to recognize truth outside of you. If you are seeing it outside of you and you just simply love that, then the same part in you begins to become enlivened without your effort through your simple, inner honesty and surrender to what that honesty reveals.

If you surrender to that inner honesty, you will find yourself loving the living truth outside of you, and that will be feeding living truth inside of you. Then it actually would not matter to you anymore who gets it, as long as someone does. If someone were to pour living truth into you or pour living truth into someone beside you, and you had a simple love of the truth, it would not make any difference which one was chosen. You would simply be loving that it poured.

If you really didn't mind that the person next door had the truth poured into them, then it sounds like you're already there, at least somewhere on that path.

All it takes for you to be like that is for you to be honest, just simply honest. Then it could not make any difference where the truth was being poured. It is only dishonesty that could possibly say: "Me instead of him." Honesty would say: "Please pour, any way, to anyone."

Is that enlightenment or awakening? Pre-awakening?

It is pre-pre-awakening. It is just honesty, really simple honesty. And to let in that kind of honesty will cause awakening.

That is not what I understand by the word honesty. Doesn't it also include a a kind of graciousness or charity?

There is no charity in it. It is just honestly not knowing where it would be most true for truth to be poured, because you do not know for which one it would be better. If you were just simply honest inside, the response would be: "I don't know." What you do know of what would be good, is for truth to pour wherever, however.

It sounds like a really surreal scenario.

But it is not. When I am connecting with people, why would you want to be connected with, if someone already is and if you know that something true is actually happening? Then, for you to be profoundly honest, you would know that truth is happening over there, and that would be good enough. To you, that would be everything, just that it is happening.

I have an idea that for truth, whatever that is, I have to wave my hands crazily and get your attention. That is my effort toward starting the receptivity process, even though I might not be completely receptive. I have to make the effort, like coming here to see you, because otherwise I could stay home and say: "There are a couple of hundred people down at the Royal National Hotel and they are being filled with truth. That is great, but I'm going to stay home and watch Coronation Street."

And that would be really good, because it would be a dissolving of your emotional attachment to needing to get what other people are getting here. And then the reason why you would come would only be because of a pull within you to come. It would not be a mental pull nor an emotional pull, just the tiniest pull of being, and that would be enough for you to come. That would be the only good, real reason to come. All the other reasons are just emotional and mental. They are reasons, but not good ones.

V. ENLIGHTENMENT THROUGH ENDARKENMENT

I saw you on Monday night and I thought: "I'm not coming back, not coming to see you, I heard it before." And I woke up on Tuesday morning and I felt: "No, I'm gonna go back," and I felt unusual, but I'm still not sure that I know what you're talking about, what you're describing, if I'm experiencing it and exactly what it is.

There is a pull of being in you that I experience, as I am knowing you.

And is it that pull that brought me here?

It is mixed.

What is the other thing?

Emotional and mental, but that part of a pull makes no difference. It is the pull of being that really brings you here. Even if it is mixed, it is still a true pull, only it is surrounded by other pulls; it is just partly illegitimate.

How can I feel the slightest pull as you describe it? How can I know what you're talking about?

You do not need to. If you are honest inside and you do not seem to understand, then it does not matter. You can rest inside without understanding. The only thing that does matter is that you can isolate something that you do know inside. And you can surrender to that. You can surrender to what you know is true.

That spiel "what I know is true" doesn't make a lot of sense to me.

Which do you know, do you really, really know is true? On the inside to hang onto something, or on the inside to let it go? Which one do you know is a living truth: to hang onto bitterness or to soften and open? Any time that you are bitter inside, there is always a pull of being, a very gentle pull that comes up to where you are in that bitterness. It pulls and it draws and it woos you to let go of what you are hanging onto.

I see two things going on: I feel relieved when bitterness goes, but I find I can call it back and feel justified that I'm bitter about something.

What if you were to become quieted and gentled inside? Then that path would end, and instead of you justifying something, you would be letting-go of something. That is a living truth. It is the same for you as it is for everybody. It is an absolute, a living absolute and it is constantly pulling inside of everyone.

There is only one living way, one kind of way of being that really lives and is really true. All the other ways of being have to be rationalized, supported, held together, defended, protected. Every other way of being requires some measure of dishonesty.

I feel like I shouldn't ask for compensation nor be involved in a legal case. Would that be correct, is that what you're talking about?

You can stand on an external right and justify something externally, for shallow reasons, but inside you would not do so. If you were to pursue litigation, it would be done shallowly and not by holding onto a right inside. It would be done with an inner openness and a softness and a rest wherein it really would not make any difference to you what the outcome would be. Either one would be okay.

Sometimes it starts off really shallow and then it becomes really serious and intense.

The moment it becomes serious and obsessive on the inside, you are so much better off to, even on the outside, let it go. If you have to close

V. ENLIGHTENMENT THROUGH ENDARKENMENT

and harden on the inside to accomplish something on the outside, then whatever it is you are accomplishing or doing, is not worth it.

That is difficult to accept.

It is a living truth. It is something that, when you are honest inside, you know is true and you know is actually really good. If you can stay wonderfully open and soft inside, then you can deal with anything outside of you in any way you like, just as long as you do not have to close and harden in order to do so. If you could stay soft and open, then you could just do as you please; it would make no difference what you did. It is never worth closing and hardening inside to accomplish something outside of you. If you could gain something like enlightenment, and all you would have to do inside is just close and harden to achieve it, then your enlightenment would be total loss and total ruin.

Are you saying it could happen like that or are you just saying if it were to happen like that it would be ruin?

If you could achieve or attain enlightenment or anything else of real value by holding onto something, it would be total ruin. And you attempt to do it that way all the time. If you could simply reach inside into your innermost being and pull up everything that is so good and so perfect, you would take that and spread it all over your whole life to make your life really nice; that is why no one can get in when there is dishonesty.

If dishonesty could access the innermost, people would corrupt themselves right to the innermost, whereas the way it is, they can only corrupt the outermost. The innermost is incorruptible. As soon as something corrupts in the outermost of consciousness, that part of consciousness is incapable of getting in. And that is good.

Did you say consciousness not getting in is good?

For outermost consciousness that is presently distorted or twisted or corrupted, it is really good that it cannot reach in toward the innermost. There is no access inside. As soon as that outermost distortion of consciousness allows itself to be honest, allows itself to undistort and untwist until it returns to an original way of being, then outermost consciousness can easily just reach straight in. But then the only reason it would reach straight in would be to simply give itself away to the innermost, without needing to get anything. The outermost would be recognizing that the innermost is worth more.

Outermost consciousness would be giving itself away to the innermost, and that would allow the innermost to move and flow into the outermost. An exchange of flow would happen. The two would become one. The two would become integrated as one. And eventually there would be no innermost and outermost anymore. Once integrated, the two would become the same; they would become a unified whole.

Has this got anything to do with following your conscience?

That is something that you never want to follow. Following your conscience is a sure way of getting away from truth. Your conscience will never show you what is true. Your conscience will only show you what you have been taught as being true, what you think is true, what society says is true and what has been patterned and ingrained in you as being true. There are many levels of conscience and all of them are, to varying degrees, useless except for the deepest one: a form of conscience that will only distinguish between whether you are actually being honest right to the core or whether you are actually being dishonest right to the core. That deepest form is the very beginning of conscience and it precedes all the levels of trained conscience. It is the very, very tiny little root. It will only tell you whether your innermost, foundational way of being, is honest or dishonest.

The further you climb up the ladder of conscience the more valueless it becomes. The higher you move into a patterned form of conscience, the sillier it is. You can even have a bad conscience about not washing your face when you get up in the morning, if this is what you have been taught. It is still conscience, but it is worthless. That sort of conscience is a value judgment and you can be trained or conditioned in ridiculous value judgments.

You actually have an amazing capacity for true value judgment, but you have to go all the way down – right to the very, very root, the very beginning of your capacity to judge values – to make a real value judgment. And the only value judgment that you can possibly make that is real and true is: core honesty is of value and true, and any kind of core dishonesty is valueless, it is untrue.

We do not like going to that fine living root of honesty of conscience. We like to climb up a few rungs to give ourselves something to play with in our consciences. We like to be pacified, and justify ourselves by saying that we are trying our best, or we are working on something. But all that really means nothing, because the focus is not taking place in the one and only place where it really counts. It is somewhere further up where it does not actually, really matter.

I'm not sure that I'm equipped to do this, to know what true honesty is and how to go forward in that.

Honesty is just a true inclination of your being. Dishonesty is you giving into something that is merely a thought, a feeling, an intuition or a desire in an effort to make yourself comfortable or happy inside. There is a true inclination of being that is very fragile, very sensitive, very weak. It will never push, never force itself, but it always gives a fine, true indication that you do not need to be comfortable and you do not need to be happy. It is always speaking to you with a very gentle touch and a soft voice: "Whatever you are presently not okay with in your thoughts and feelings, your intuition, body and will, is on the inside, actually okay; you can easily and very gently let it go."

CHAPTER 6

Tender Honesty is a Cure-All

You are consciousness.
You have a full spectrum of consciousness.
What is within you is
the greatest power in the universe.
You can choose.

Nobody chooses for you – you get to choose.
You get to be
true to your innermost,

or you get to be true to
what you want to be true,
what you need to be true.

You get to choose
your own truth,
or you can surrender to
the only truth.

The greatest power
in the universe
is in you.
It is all in you.

VI. TENDER HONESTY IS A CURE-ALL

Questioner: This year my marriage broke down. It was only once we were separated that I was suddenly faced with the numbness, shock, and the pain that I am causing those around me. I am trying to understand my part throughout the marriage and over the last six months. I don't know if there is anything I need to do or be? I don't even know if I am meant to be continuing in this marriage.

John: The end of your marriage or the state that it is presently in, actually reflects the core, the real core of how you went into marriage.

We got married because I was pregnant.

Aside from that – that has nothing to do with it. That is shallow, that is superficial. That does not really, deeply mean anything. You went into marriage for you. That is what ruined it, because marriage is not for you. Marriage is for your innermost being; for the living essence of truth to have a place to express itself with another being. It's for truth, not for you.

It does not matter how you start a marriage: how incredibly in love you are, how bonded you are, how perfect it is, how well it works, how compatible you are. All of that means little. It will not last, because you will ruin it. When you are in love, it is all so good, it is so even, and there is so much there that makes you happy. You found everything that you ever looked for. But when you find all of that for you, the marriage is already falling apart. It only takes time for you to realize how deeply that is true. The way that the marriage ends up shows how you really began it.

If you were to have the worst imaginable marriage, that would be a good start. That would be a really wonderful start because then everything you could see would really be as is. You would be seeing all of your wants and your needs not being satisfied. There would be a recognition that what you thought and felt and hoped a marriage should be is not at all what is there. And recognizing that, you would be standing on the doorstep of seeing what a real marriage is all about.

When you begin with a really wonderful marriage, a nice marriage, a good marriage, then you have an illusion that it is actually good, that it really satisfies, that there is something real there, but that is not so. When the goodness you are seeing is for your happiness, then your eyes are closed to what is really there. You are only seeing the outermost satisfaction of your wants and your needs. The truth of that marriage has not yet been realized as consciousness, because the innermost of consciousness has not been addressed. You as consciousness have not been in the marriage for truth. You as consciousness have only come to know the marriage for you.

When a marriage starts out rotten, your eyes are open and you can see. That is a wonderful start for a marriage, because all you need to do is let in just a very tender okayness. Let the marriage be as is, that it never needs to change for you but that it can change. That you will let yourself rest inside of that marriage as is, without it ever needing to be fixed. That you, with gentleness and tenderness, will be wonderfully okay just to be in that marriage, and that it is not at all for the you you are familiar with. Will you be in the marriage only for the okayness that is deep within you, only so that real living okayness has a place to express itself right from your innermost all the way through you? Will you allow innermost rest to show up in this rotten marriage and just be in it?

The only value any marriage has, is you being that okay with it, as is. If you are that okay with your marriage as is, then you will be that accepting of your husband. Nothing in him will ever need to change for you – he is okay, as is. It will be warm inside of you that he really does not need to change.

For your way of being to change and transform into okayness out of not-okayness, a flow would be moving from within you and out through you. It would be an energy with no grip in it; it would not be looking to get anything. There would be no grabbing, no getting. It would be an energy of rest, of okayness and acceptance, flowing only to be okay. Everything that it touched would be with gentle rest, acceptance and

VI. TENDER HONESTY IS A CURE-ALL

okayness. Everything that it touched would heal, without even trying.

What that would do to your husband is one of two things. It would cause an incredible pull for him to meet the response coming from his own being to that kind of energy in you. He would want to meet the response within himself and completely give into it, because it is so irresistible, so good. It is everything that he has ever, honestly been looking for. Or, he would become hardened, because he would refuse to live with this kind of energy. He would insist on being supremely not okay and not bend for anything. And then he would become even more miserable, or he would be gone.

You have the best marriage to start out with. You no longer have to be in the marriage for you: to be happy, to be comfortable, to feel okay, to get what you want, to be loved. You do not need any of that. You do not need to be loved because you can be okay with him as is. He does not need to love you, not for you. You can be okay with his love, and you can also be just as okay without his love.

For there to be no preference, you would be in a state of innocence. You would not choose between one and the other, not strive for one or the other. And because you would not choose, prefer or strive, you would be equally present in a true way of being, whether he loved you or not. There would be nothing in you for him to touch or grab; the buttons he might push would be gone. The only thing that he could possibly touch inside of you would be innocence, cleanness and okayness.

To take a step right through into a sexual relationship with him would be quite a leap.

If you are that okay, that would cause a totally different kind of sexual flow. Instead of just chemistry moving and hormones moving, what would be moving through your being and your sexuality would be your innermost essence. That essence of living truth moving from your innermost consciousness would provoke opening and softening. It would provoke newness. There would be no pull to get something. There would be no inner resistance, no trying to keep something out. There would be a flow of innocence and tender okayness through sexuality, a healing flow through sexuality. Sexuality is for that depth of okayness in you to express itself. Sexuality is not for the you that you think and feel you are.

The more you try to use sexuality for you, the more dissatisfying it becomes. The greater the experiences on the surface, the less satisfying they will be, really, really deep within, in the stillness of innermost consciousness. Sexuality in marriage is for living truth; the innermost essence within you as consciousness to have a place to express itself, a place to manifest itself in. It is for the real you. It is not for the you that you are accustomed to. It is for your innermost being. And your entire life is for your being. None of it is for you.

Now you finally have a really wonderful start in marriage. And your husband will, with this kind of energy, either really despise you and even leave you to protect himself from your inner tenderness that enlivens and re-acquaints him with the same tenderness within himself, or he will really love you, not because of you, but because there is something flowing from you that he knows, something so new and so clean that touches exactly the same place and the same way of being inside of him. And then a union and a merge of being will begin to happen between you and your husband. Neither one of you will use that for yourselves. You will not keep it for you. You will give that away to the place from which it came, simply be being in it in the same way, through openness and surrender.

In a way there is nothing for me to actually say or force to make a shift – it's more a question of where I'm coming from or just how I am. My husband said I needed to make a change of heart for it to work and I said I didn't know how things would be and evolve over the next few months.

Now you know. You as your heart or as consciousness can go within, and everything that you find there that is not okay, you can finally be

VI. TENDER HONESTY IS A CURE-ALL

at rest with. Changing your whole heart is so easy. But if you try to change just a little portion of your heart to make something okay inside while the remainder is living from a place of not-okayness, then that remainder will never put up with you letting in the only thing that will ruin it. You will be torn on the inside, and there will not be rest.

If your whole heart is letting in okayness – allowing innermost rest to go into any corner inside, into any kind of construct and attachment, allowed to simply be that rest anywhere inside of you – then changing your heart is so easy. It will happen all by itself. It is a very simple healing. It is living to remain in openness and softness on the inside, with anything that causes pain or that you do not understand on the outside. And you can remain in that way of being, that innermost rest that warmly disarms your use of any judgment and warmly disarms your protection of anything you were holding onto.

Where there is simple okayness inside, there is no judgment. Love happens, a kind of love that has no conditions to it, has no end; a kind of love that cannot be pushed over the edge. It would not matter how deeply you went into it, you could never get to the end. It is a kind of love that has no lines in it. There are no lines of non-acceptance and if there were pressure, you would always allow that in and be at rest with it, inside. Your greatest treasure would be that you get to remain warmly okay, with absolutely anything.

That is your living treasure. That is something that flows directly from your innermost and you get to surrender to it. There is nothing that can stop you from surrendering to it. You get to live that way, no matter what kind of discomfort, no matter what kind of not-okayness there is. Nothing can stop you from surrendering to your innermost and letting your innermost flow through and occupy all of your space. It can have your whole life: your marriage, your children, your friends, all of your opportunities. It can have your entire future.

And your greatest delight will be that okayness gets to have you, that you get to live for it instead of you looking for okayness to have for yourself for a feel-good. It is easy and it is so simple, as long as you leave you out of the equation. Leave every issue out and let openness and softness in. You will be as clear inside as you were when you were a little baby, and that same kind of clean, innocent, nurturing flow will begin to move. You were once like that. You worked yourself out of it, and it is really easy to just simply let yourself back in. A rotten marriage is a wonderful one; it is where just the tiniest little bit of innermost essence shines so brightly.

All our surface bodies seem redundant until we are in a state of enlightenment, when they can be used to expand and extend beingness into the physical world. It seems almost like a cruelty of nature or God, whoever created this physical form with all these surface bodies, to create something that's going to be in the way of us being in beingness.

Nothing stands in the way of your beingness. Your surface bodies or vehicles, in their present condition with all of their dysfunctions, are your nearest opportunities to beingness. Your surface vehicles are closest to you, in form, for you as consciousness to dwell inside of.

For you to be okay with your distorted emotional vehicle as it presently is, without ever needing to change it, then you as consciousness would have something to dwell in from a way of being that originates from your innermost - from a way of being that is true. You as consciousness would get to, with tender okayness, be inside of something that does not feel okay.

The only cruelty that exists is when consciousness lets in dishonesty – when consciousness functions in a way of being that it actually knows is not true. That is the only real cruelty that exists. Every other cruelty that we recognize in form is just the result of this one.

I was thinking in particular of the intellectual body. If someone who is intellectual completely goes into a mind space where they're rationalizing ...

That is not an intellectual, that is a pseudo-intellectual.

VI. TENDER HONESTY IS A CURE-ALL

I feel it's much harder for someone like that to be okay, because he or she can just go on a big mind trip.

Not if that person is honest. Honesty stops that short. Honesty is the knife of reality that cuts through everything that is untrue. There is nothing that honesty cannot penetrate and go straight through and make okay. Honesty of being is true pain relief for the mental vehicle. Honesty of being is true pain relief for the emotional vehicle because what it brings is simple, warm, innermost rest.

Pain is just the unraveller of tension. Allow okayness or innermost rest into the mental vehicle. That will instantaneously start an evenness that will keep spreading through the whole of the mental vehicle until it eventually becomes healed, becomes whole. Then there will be no such thing as a deep problem. Find a problem anywhere and just let some honesty into it. It will no longer be a problem, it will be something that is warmly okay.

What you teach reflects what the Buddha taught, which was about total acceptance of what is. But he said we should become enlightened through meditating and experiencing the profound okayness that you talk about, so why is it that you say no to meditating?

How do you know the Buddha said that? Why believe that he said that?

Why believe that you are enlightened?

You do not have to believe that I am enlightened. You need only believe the littlest bit inside of you, that you honestly and really do know is true. That you can believe. And if what I say happens to touch that knowing in you, then you can believe that touch because it moves what you are already knowing inside of you. There is no point in pleasing me.

Something in me is touched, but I'm resisting. I resist someone who is, I feel, in some way claiming to be reflecting truth. In my mind I feel you are reflecting a truth. I feel okay if you say, this is a way, a truth, but not when you say this is "the truth".

Only honesty knows the truth. Dishonesty has lots of truths, and none of them work. There is only one living way of being and it is exactly the same way for everyone. There is only one way of being that truly works. Only one way of being represents innermost consciousness, your innermost being, and that living way is the same absolute living truth for everyone else.

Is it not possible that there are different ways to be in that living truth, to come into that living truth?

In terms of the way of being on the inside, there is only one way.

I'm speaking more about the way to getting there. Do I meditate or do I not? Do I read, do I not?

Why not let a complete and a total honesty give you the answer, instead of going into your mind to get the answer? Your mental vehicle will only tell you what you have already put into it in terms of what you want to be true and what you need to be true. If there is any measure of dishonesty inside of you, your mind will support that. It will never support honesty, it will never support truth. The only time that your mind will support honesty and truth is if you, as consciousness are letting yourself be simply honest all the way through the mind and all of your surface vehicles, at any cost.

I don't know what that is.

When you are in a quieted and gentled place on the inside, what do you really know about meditation?

I don't really know.

Then how can you meditate?

When I am in meditation, I experience acceptance and I can bring that into my life. I experience okayness.

Then meditation was like a vehicle – it happened to be what you were in when you came in touch with your innermost. But it was not the meditation that did it. What actually did it was you touching your innermost through honesty while you were meditating. The moment honesty lets you touch the innermost, you can immediately let go of the attachment to the meditation and continue to go through the door that you entered when you happened to be meditating. To keep meditating is like staying inside of the door. You do not need the entrance, you just need to go in.

It seems to me that meditation is like a state of being, the beingness that you spoke about.

If meditation is a state of being, then why associate meditation with techniques for the mind? Why include those in the package? Inasmuch as meditation is a technique, then you can let that go.

I can accept the point of not being attached to it, but I can't accept that it's not useful.

Anything is useful: meditation, reading a book, going for a walk, watching a movie. Anything that you can possibly do in this life is useful because if there is honesty inside, even when you are watching a movie, then something will pierce or move you within. Your own innermost being will begin to open up and flow because of your honesty while watching that movie.

All activity is useful inasmuch as it is an opportunity for honesty to be in instead of a tool for you to get something. The only real value lies in the way of being in that activity, not the activity itself.

And when you spoke about not having an ego, did you mean that you don't experience pain and you don't have reactions? What did you mean by that?

Being without ego is living in a way that has no dishonesty generating a personal agenda.

When you say agenda, is that wanting something?

An agenda is living from a place of want or need. It is living from a place of non-acceptance, living from a space of not-okayness. The ego only comes out of not-okayness. That is where it originates. The ego will only represent not-okayness. It can only represent what it came out of. It can only represent its own source. If you are no longer living in the source from which the ego came, then the only thing that can live is what comes out of a different source. If that source is truth, and all of you as consciousness moves from that source and lives for that source, then there is no ego.

Can you say that in a different way?

If you are living from the source that you really come from, then there is no ego in that source. If you create a different source, one that you actually know is not true, then that source is illusion. When you live for illusion, ego springs out of that to protect itself and the illusion. The ego is just illusion working for itself and being supported by you as consciousness.

VI. TENDER HONESTY IS A CURE-ALL

If you no longer give energy to want and need, to something that you want to be true and need to be true, then any illusion that you have put together, that you are presently living in, begins to dissolve and fall apart, as though it never was. And all that remains is the real you. Then there is nothing for the ego to live in anymore, because the ego was a part of that illusion. When the illusion is let go of, the ego dies. When the need of living inside of any amount of illusion ends, then the source of ego ends. The life of the ego is dependent on a lie being sustained.

Why does consciousness support it?

Consciousness supporting an illusion is consciousness choosing to believe something that it wants to be true, even though it actually knows it is not true. It is consciousness lying to itself.

So you are not talking about pure consciousness?

I am referring to dishonest consciousness. Consciousness can be dishonest. Consciousness can believe something and make it true, even though it is just a perception. Consciousness can take a dream and say: "This is my truth, this is my reality, this is what I live for." And there will be an ego that rises out of that to protect the dream. That ego is consciousness living through the dream, through the illusion. If consciousness ceases to believe in a lie, then ego ends. But that takes a kind of honesty within consciousness that is complete, in a way that the whole of consciousness is one with what actually, really, really is, and no longer one with what it wants to be true.

If there is dishonesty, there is a split in consciousness – a split between what you know is true and what you want to be true. Then you are living in an illusion and your consciousness exists in a state of separation. The outermost of consciousness is separated and pulled away from the innermost. But the innermost continues to move and continues to touch that dishonest form of consciousness that has separated itself.

The innermost of consciousness always remains connected even through the separation. There is always a pull. There is always a pull to go back home, to return to that oneness and return to that completeness. But if there is any insistence in consciousness anywhere to have what it wants to be true, then it holds itself separate. It tries to prove that the truth it wants to be true is true. It will live its life manifesting its own truth. But everything it touches and everything it does, will not work. And within that separated form of consciousness there will be a perpetual ache. There will be a perpetual ache because consciousness actually knows that it is not being whole and complete like the innermost, and that everything it does is not whole and complete either.

The only thing that is it – the only thing that brings a kind of peace that is complete, a joy that is true, a love that is real – is when that separated consciousness just simply lets go of what it is holding onto and returns to the whole, when it will be as the innermost. Then there is a oneness of consciousness with no separation. In that state, in that way of being, there is no ego. When consciousness is separated, holding itself apart from the rest, there is ego.

And if one is profoundly okay with that, can that be the oneness of consciousness?

When one is profoundly okay with that, then that separated form of consciousness begins to return. There is a little feeler that goes to the pure, original, innermost of consciousness and touches that. As soon as it touches that, a resonance moves all the way through the separated part of consciousness and causes an incredible pull for the rest to come as well.

As that touch of what comes from the innermost of consciousness moves up into your mental vehicle, you begin to realize the implications of what this is going to cost you. You realize that there is a little part of you as consciousness that is surrendering to the innermost source, and that that little part is honest. But the rest of you as consciousness holds out, waiting to see what is going to happen. If it is too dangerous, it will pull away. If it is far too dangerous, it will even pull back that little bit of honesty back into the ego.

If consciousness stays honest, it will let that feeler go and touch, and with one touch there will be an incredible resonance that comes back. There will be a profound satisfaction of being that says: "It's true, it's real." And when consciousness responds to that little touch, then more of consciousness will begin to allow itself to touch the innermost as well.

When consciousness is being honest, then everything touching what is true stays; it never comes back, it never retracts. Finally, there will be so many feelers going out, that all of the separated forms of consciousness will end up back home and there will be oneness. The only price that consciousness had to pay was to let go of everything that took it away in the first place; it let go of everything that it thought it gained while it was away from its innermost. That is all you will lose. All you lose is everything.

Why, when you were enlightened years ago, did you lose that?

What happened was that there was a feeler that was pulled to the source. And I lived inside of that feeler. And it so happened that ...

What's a feeler?

A feeler is a little bit of consciousness returning home. It was what I lived inside of for a year, and not inside of the separated part which simply remained there as well. It was not until real pressure hit, that I retracted. I pulled back the little feeler which was my living connection to my innermost of consciousness. And then the experience of being completely home was instantaneously gone.

Then I began to search, because now I knew that I had experienced the real thing. And I knew that I could not live until I had gotten it back, until I had not only found it, but found the real source of what was happening. And I wanted to find it with understanding.

At first, I tried every dishonest way possible inside. As a thief I tried everything. None of it worked. And then, I let myself be completely honest. I let honesty go right to the core of that separated part and a oneness began to happen with the innermost, without any effort at all. I was responding in a true way of openness and softness of being, to the innermost of the separated part of consciousness which had once been part of the whole. In responding that way, I was actually resonating with its source, because I was being in the same way as the source. I was letting myself resonate with the innermost source. So I actually became as the innermost source through the simplest form of honesty. That started the re-connection. That was the beginning of a true homecoming.

The more that I experienced pressure – pressure inside of this world, pressure from within my surface vehicles to retract inside as consciousness and to separate, pressure to look for a way out of pain and to look for a way of securing happiness for myself – the more I continued to be as honest as I possibly could be. The oneness continued and just went deeper and deeper and deeper. There was nothing that I would not let go of. It did not matter what the pressure was, I remained honest and allowed that honesty to go deeper, become finer and finer.

What started to open up was an incredible depth of being. There was transformation after transformation after transformation. As the depth of being began to open up, I started to become intimately acquainted with my innermost, deeper and deeper and deeper and deeper.

When you are living from the innermost of consciousness, there is no ego. There is only an ease of living truth. It is really as easy for you to be completely home inside, as it is for truth itself. The only way that it might be difficult is if you are not being honest.

I'm obviously not being honest, but I don't know how I am not being honest.

Has there been any bitterness?

VI. TENDER HONESTY IS A CURE-ALL

There have been subtle reactions, subtle discomfort.

Has there been any measure of hanging onto it? Has there been any hesitation in letting it go? Has there been any hesitation at all when something grabbed a hold of you, in letting it go? The moment there is just a touch of hesitation to let go, there is dishonesty. When there is insistence on something, then there is real dishonesty. And when you begin justifying and rationalizing it, then honesty is a long way away.

You can live perpetually letting-go inside, in such a way that you will not hang onto something inside for any reason; you cannot be bought inside. There will be nothing meaningful enough for which you will say: "Well for that I would consider hanging on," or: "To get rid of that amount of pain, I would consider hanging on."

When there is honesty, a core honesty, you cannot be bought. Nothing can buy you. You have no price. It does not matter how much is offered in reward or pain relief, does not matter how great that package is, you would never even consider having it and being dishonest to get it. There is nothing that could buy you into holding onto something inside. You would be open and soft within and live that way, in the midst of this world. Nothing could make you hold on inside. Nothing could make you harden inside. You would perpetually let everything in and everything through. You would always be as you actually know is true: one simple way of being that is constant openness and softness. That is honesty. All it takes is a little bit of pressure and what is really there will reveal itself.

You are consciousness. You have a full spectrum of consciousness. What is within you is the greatest power in the universe – you can choose. No one chooses for you. You get to choose. You get to be true to your innermost, or you get to be true to what you want to be true, what you need to be true. You get to choose your own truth, or you can surrender to the only truth. The greatest power in the universe is in you.

It is all in you. You have that kind of clarity. You have that kind of power. You have no excuse for not being home. You have no excuse for not being okay, because it is all in you. It has nothing to do with anything outside of you. It really does not have anything to do with your mind, your emotions or your body. It has only to do with you as consciousness: whether you are actually fully surrendering to what you know is true, or whether you are in some little way, surrendering to something that you want to be true and going outside of your true self to do it.

If you are going outside of your true self, life becomes difficult, because it does not matter what you touch and what you do, it will never work; there is no reality in it. There is no innermost in a dishonest touch. Then everything that you try to do is something of a lie, something of a want and something of a need. There is not a congruency between what you are touching and doing, and your innermost. There is a separation. And what is doing that is just you. This genius of consciousness that has the power to actually make something up, believe in it, and live in it as though it were really true. And what is so wonderful is that it never works.

As consciousness you never get away with it. There is no escape from being at one with what is real. As soon as you are not at one with what is real, you will be profoundly not okay. All that you do in life will, on the inside, never work. And that is so good. And you always have a mirror; every moment in life is a reality check. Every moment in life is telling you it is not working. Consciousness is so awesome!

John, what are your thoughts about mental health? I'm quite interested in doing some work with people who are suffering from schizophrenia, depression and things like that.

There is one really, really simple cure to every form of mental and emotional illness, and that is honesty; honesty followed by a clear giving in, a clear surrender to what one actually, really knows is true. That will heal any kind of mental and emotional illness. There is no mental illness anywhere that can withstand honesty.

But honesty still comes from the higher self bringing the honesty through

VI. TENDER HONESTY IS A CURE-ALL

the rest of the body. Where is the honesty recognized? How does that person recognize they're in honesty?

Everyone knows about honesty. Everyone knows how powerful it is, what kind of healer it is. We know it so well, that we actually cover it up and create a system or a confusion inside, so that we can say in our mind, that we do not know how to be honest. We know that if we were to let ourselves really see just a tiny little bit of that real honesty, its power would immediately pierce through everything. And everything that honesty touched would instantly heal.

You're working now by assisting new people to know honesty.

You cannot truly move people and really affect their knowing, their honesty, unless you are absolutely honest yourself. If you are not home, there is a shifty energy that comes out of you. There is a genius at work that can take something and turn it into something that it is not. If you are not home, that deceptive energy is coming through.

So if you are working with mental patients and you are trying to show them through your own dishonesty how to be honest, then your energy will be very relieving to them. They will listen to what you are saying, let it all in, side with the part of you that is dishonest, and then their own dishonesty will have just been reinforced. Their dishonesty will have been justified and fortified and now they will be even less inclined to be honest or be healed.

Everything you do in life, none of it will work unless you are home. It is not just a career, it is relationships, it is everything you touch, everything you do, everything that you are present in throughout your entire life. None of it will work unless you are home. What is true is not to stop living until you are home. What is true is just go home and keep living.

Are you saying that as kind of a warning, or should one just go ahead and try to do the work anyway if one is not home?

You can go ahead and be homeless. You can go ahead and keep doing the work from a place that is at least somewhat not home. And then what is so good is that you will reap what you sow. It will not truly work.

What about getting the person to see their wonder, see their godliness, their spirit within them?

Only honesty can see. Dishonest people cannot see their own true, innermost beauty. They can only see what they think and what they feel, while that innermost beauty remains deep within. They cannot really see that beauty. But honesty can go right inside, directly access the true innermost beauty, immerse itself in it, bathe in it and live in it.

Anything originating from dishonesty can never get in, can never find it. Dishonesty can only find what is not true, can only find a lie that it made up. Dishonesty can never find the truth. It can never find innermost essence, cleanness, clarity or okayness. Dishonesty can only find trying and striving and doing and working and labouring – it can only find not-okayness. And all dishonesty will ever do is keep trying to fix it.

I guess the first thing required before a person acquires honesty, is being in a safe place.

That is conditional honesty. People will do that. There are people who will let everything open up while they are walking through nature. They will be really honest because they feel safe. But as soon as they no longer feel safe they close up, protect themselves and live inside of a space of dishonesty.

In practical terms, how would you get past that?

VI. TENDER HONESTY IS A CURE-ALL

Easily, because I am living in a space that is already past their block. I am already inside of them as consciousness. I am already one with the innermost part of them, that is always in a way of letting-go. As consciousness I move with their own innermost being through to the outside of consciousness to tenderly persuade and move and woo their honesty.

That was what I was trying to get at regarding working with the higher part of a person.

But if you are not completely home then you will attempt to do this with other people, for you. That is where there is a craftiness. That is why anytime there is any measure of dishonesty, then any part of you that is not home is a thief. And that part that is not home gets into everything. There is nothing that dishonesty cannot access, except your innermost.

With regard to anything that you are doing with people, any part of you that is not home has its fingers right in it and is getting exactly what it wants. It can make itself look very loving. It can be very righteous. The only thing it cannot afford to be is honest; it will not let itself. If it is honest, then everything that it is holding is immediately let go of. It falls apart, and there is a melting right into the innermost.

So a place of honesty would be a place of not caring about the outcome, a place of non-attachment to the outcome?

It is being genuinely free of the outcome. You can only be genuinely free of the outcome if you are actually tenderly resting in a place that is true. If you are in a place that is true, in a place that is honest and clean right to the innermost, then you have want of nothing. You have need of nothing, because everything is presently complete and there is nothing that you could bring in from the outside that could make it even a tiny little bit better or more complete. It is already whole. Living in a way of honesty is most wonderfully being free of any coarse attachment to or wishing for an outcome – an outcome you know has nothing to do with what you are in love with most.

If everything is already perfect anyway, then you're cutting off the need to be doing anything in the first place.

That is right. Then you will not need to be a helper anymore. Then anything that you do is just play, and you only do it because in a true way, you can. It is all a flow manifesting what you are presently being inside. You will not be a helper. You will not be here to love people back to life. You will not be here to change the world. You will not be here to change anyone. You will actually only be here just to really, truly be. And it will be totally clean. Without any effort at all, that will heal everything around you. You will exist as a true source of healing and you will never touch it, because it is not for you. It is so easy and so lovely.

It is as if the whole of my life revolves around simply trying to protect this little physical body from death because I'm scared of dying and I don't know what's on the other side of that veil. I know it seems so profoundly and deeply dishonest to live just to protect these little body things that don't seem to mean anything, yet I don't know how to release the identification with this body so that I'm not afraid of death. Then I would be living for some other purpose. But all I'm aware of now is I'm just this bundle of fear and terror that knows if it doesn't get up in the morning, doesn't go to work, it's going to die.

That is not all you know.

That's all I honestly know.

That is all you think you know. It is not all you do know. You have already experienced life after death. Anytime you have let something die inside of you – some kind of not-okayness, something that you were

VI. TENDER HONESTY IS A CURE-ALL

hanging onto, some little bit of illusion, dishonesty, insistence, some measure of bitterness, hardness, closedness or hatred – anytime that you have simply let that issue die by letting-go, what you found of life after death was okayness. You experienced tiny, tiny little tastes of what it is all about.

I am aware of these tiny little tastes, but it seems to me that ninety-nine percent of my life is devoted to running away from fear of the big death. I know that there are times when I let go and there is a little releasing or letting-go of something, but it seems so trivial in comparison to the whole basis of my life.

Then take that little bit that seems so trivial, which actually lives, and let it loose. Let it go anywhere it would choose. Let it touch any issue that it is moved to touch and let it choose which issues it will, in tenderness, touch first. Let honesty loose, let it have anything. Let okayness loose, let it go anywhere. Okayness, if you let it loose, will make everything simple and profoundly okay.

Even my living to survive death, even that? It feels so profound. There is this intense fear of what lies on the other side.

I have come back from death. Within myself, I have allowed the same dying of illusion, dishonesty and not-okayness that you are presently speaking of. And what I am as a way of being is, to your core, rather comforting.

In regard to you coming back from the dead, you weren't living in illusion, but I'm still living in ninety-nine percent illusion.

That is okay, because I have touched that one percent that is not. The other ninety-nine percent are wonderfully meaningless. I will not touch the ninety-nine percent in you. I have no attachment to the ninety-nine percent in you. But I am wonderfully attached to that one percent in you. There is an attachment of being, a bond of being. It is through that bond that I know exactly how to find your innermost, touch your innermost, and allow you to know that the one percent is real, and is not an illusion.

I am aware that there must be something that is real. But because I live my life through the other ninety-nine percent, then ninety-nine percent of the time I feel like I'm just a worm – dishonest to the core.

You are not dishonest to the core. You are ninety-nine percent dishonest to the core. The one percent that is honest, that one tiny little bit where you will actually let yourself see what you know is real, that is what you love. When you see that, it touches you, nourishes you. That tiny little bit that you see is like nectar; it represents healing. That is the only part in you that matters.

To me, honesty means not paying attention to that one percent, but paying attention to the rest of the ninety-nine percent. Honesty is looking at all the dark stuff and facing it head on.

Honesty is not facing the dark stuff. Honesty is not facing anything head on. Honesty is you going inside of that one percent in you that is true, and from that one percent, looking anywhere within the ninety-nine percent. What you will be encountering head on is the one percent. You will be looking, but through the eyes of the one percent.

Then a shift will begin to happen. The one percent will become two, the two percent will become more and so on, until finally there will be a raging fire of reality inside. It is honesty that will be zooming through you, and what will be happening is you awakening. There is no amount of dishonesty that can withstand any amount of honesty.

You do not need to figure out your fears. Just look at that tiniest little bit that is presently alive and nourishing you – that is clear and real. Then give yourself to it. The lies and the illusions, they do not even matter. Fears do not matter. There is no fear that can live or be present inside of that one percent. That is the only place where fear dies.

You can take everything that you are and pour it into that little one percent, and that little one percent will become larger and larger and larger. It will become the whole, so that there will be one hundred percent of what that one percent once was. Illusions are not a problem; really tender honesty is a cure-all. Let that little bit of tender honesty, just let it touch something inside of you. See what happens.

I'm not sure that I know exactly what that one percent even is.

Is there any part of you, any space inside of you, regardless of how little, where you are just gentled and quieted inside? Is there any place inside of you where there is a space that is genuinely refreshing, just even a little bit; a kind of inner refreshment that is not connected to anything outside of you?

There is something when I stop rushing around maniacally, just sit down and allow myself to be settled and in meditation.

Then while you are meditating, or while you are being quiet, as soon as that touch happens, give into that touch. Really let it in. The way that you let it into you is by you going into it. Anything that you are hanging onto, that keeps you from going in. Just let it go and go in.

How do you know when you are actually being honest with yourself? We have all this conditioning and it is quite confusing to know what is real.

How often are you hanging onto something on the inside, that you do not want to let go of? That is dishonesty. When you are hanging onto something on the inside, there is an ever present pull from your innermost being to just sweetly let it go.

But how do you know when you're hanging on? Is it when it's really difficult to let go of something?

It is when you want to, and you do not want to. The wanting to is the part of you that has a softness and an openness in it. Relinquish the neediness in wanting to let go. Then the openness and softness that remain will be letting-go-ness itself. That part of you is then clear. The part of you that does not want to let go is the part of you that is not clear. Being honest is siding with the clarity and being true to what you actually, really do know is true. Honesty is letting yourself be true to that, letting yourself side with that.

Sometimes I don't want that, because I don't want to believe the truth. That's when my head comes in and I get confused.

You not wanting to side with what you actually know is true, is you wanting to defend your own rights. It is some kind of right inside getting touched. Then, there is an insistence that that right is worth something, when it is not. A right has shallow value, but there is no right anywhere that has deep and true value. Hanging onto something inside is giving energy to a right. When you are bitter with someone or bitter about a circumstance, it is because you are deeply believing inside that a right belongs to you. You are believing that something is taking that right away from you and that you are not getting what you want. Hanging on inside is just you investing yourself in the idea that something is in the way of your happiness. If you were to have no rights inside, not one, you would be free. The more rights you acquire inside, the more you have to live to protect them.

Then wouldn't I become very vulnerable, allowing people to walk all over me?

You can use rights on the outside; you can work with rights in your

VI. TENDER HONESTY IS A CURE-ALL

shallow, surface life, but not inside. If you are quieted inside, there is always a knowing that everything is okay, that there are no rights. If someone hurts you, and you are quieted inside, you always know that on the inside, it is truly okay.

That does not mean that you need to let people hurt you on the outside or that you have to stay in abusive circumstances. But whatever is happening in the moment, inside it is okay. In the moment, inside there is no right worth hanging onto. As soon as you have a right that you are living for on the inside, then you have become a doer. You have to do, you have to labour, you have to strive to maintain something that you are believing in and you have to protect yourself.

Protecting yourself on the outside, that will not hurt you. Protecting yourself on the inside, that will really wound you. Everything is worth tenderly letting in on the inside: pain, mistreatment, abuse. Trying to keep something away from your innermost, because of disliking pain, wanting to be happy or not wanting to be hurt, still gives no real protection from internal pain. We always look for that kind of protection, but we never truly find it, because it does not exist. What we then use most to protect ourselves from internal pain is anger. We use bitterness, hatred and hardness. And when we let that in, we die inside.

If you are free inside, and if you want to change something on the outside in a circumstance or in a relationship, then you can progress on the outside with focus in changing it, so long as you are not attached to the outcome. But as soon as it really matters to you that something has to be a certain way, then you are staying inside of need, want, insistence or anger. The more you discover that what you are trying to change does not work, the deeper you will be taking in the dishonest insistence and it will never work.

It seems to me that you're telling us not to be human. But we are human, so we are going to feel and do and be all these things?

What is human? Most of what we define as being human is based on a way of being that is dishonest. It is based on a way of being that we know is not real. When you are bitter, is that being human?

I don't know. I just think that all the different feelings that everybody has are part of being a human being.

If you look at everything in this world as it presently is, is that a manifestation of what balanced humanness is? True humanness is the innermost peace that we all know about. True humanness is the kind of peace that cannot be disturbed by any thought, feeling, experience or any circumstance. That is really human.

Why are we not like that?

We place value on our own personal happiness. We make that supreme, so then we live for that and we exist to be happy. And yet happiness is not at all what we need. Responding to what we actually know is true – that is worth living for. Our own personal happiness is not worth living for. It is the want and need of happiness that ruins people. Instead of trying to be happy, which is difficult, you can simply be profoundly okay.

Okayness is human. The pursuit of happiness is inhuman; it is not what we really are and it does not work. The only genuinely happy person is the person who is unconditionally and warmly okay with not being happy. That is a truly happy person.

So that's what you are?

I am perpetually happy, even though it is something that I am not hanging onto. I do not need it, I am not looking for it nor wanting it, it just keeps happening. It is a fruit of being profoundly and unconditionally okay. It is something that people cannot get, something people cannot hang onto for themselves.

VI. TENDER HONESTY IS A CURE-ALL

If you are truly okay without happiness, it grows on its own. There is nothing that can stop it. But as soon as you need it, you cannot have it. If you acquire only a shallow or self-gratifying emotional happiness, that is dangerous, because it means you have an emotional button that can be pushed. As soon as someone touches that or crosses that or disturbs that emotional happiness, you will become very unhappy. It was not real happiness, because it could be disturbed.

Real happiness cannot be disturbed. Real happiness does not need to be held together, or protected, or looked for. It comes from within, not from the outside. Real happiness is a fruit of being. It is true inner contentment flowing from a way of being that sides absolutely and unconditionally with what it knows is true, regardless of the circumstance, regardless of any personal cost. Real happiness is the enjoyment of being tenderly okay, as is.

CHAPTER 7

That Still Small Voice

Whatever you lose
was never yours,
and whatever you could possibly gain
will never be for you.

In reality there is
no room for you.
There is only
room for your being.
That makes it really easy.

All of your work is over.
And what will happen is
your being will take over.
It will be
where you used to be.

The you that you were
trying to hold together
will all pass away,
and the real you
will finally live.

VII. THAT STILL SMALL VOICE

Questioner: Something started happening for me last night and I've been feeling quite shaky ever since. You were connecting with someone and I felt this warmth and then it locked in my chest and I felt this real constriction and tightness. All this morning it's been building up. I feel my heart is beating like it's just going to burst; I feel shaky and like there's an elephant sitting on my chest. Somehow it feels like I can't connect with you through it.

John: That is what it is there for: to protect you from connecting, protect you from remaining open and soft within, protect you from merging with what you know is true. If you remained that vulnerable, something would burst inside. And you would not be in control of that burst. So then you use a constriction as a filter to keep yourself from openness and softness, from what seems to be too much because it may profoundly disturb something you are holding together inside.

On one level I want that more than anything else. I can't see any point in not being open like that, but the mechanisms that are in place just seem so subtle. Every time I unravel part of it I come up against something else that's just as hard and immovable.

You are coming up against everything that you have ever put together to protect yourself inside – everything you have put together inside to stop the flow of reality, of truth. But now you are encountering and connecting with a powerful flow outside of you that resonates with the tiny little flow inside of you. And then all of you inside yearns to connect with that flow outside of you. But there are all these constrictions and filters in place that you have used to protect yourself during your life. If you give any energy to them at all, they will stand in the way of giving you everything that you have always truly yearned for. When there is inner conflict, it is because there is a true yearning and at the same time, a protecting yourself from the very thing that you are yearning for.

So to deal with this constriction or weight, I just need to be okay with it?

Let yourself, on the inside, simply be at rest with your protective mechanisms, at rest with your constriction and your filters, as is. Be warmly okay with those mechanisms seemingly ruining everything. Just stay wide open on the inside. As soon as you want those protective devices to go away, that will make them stronger. Any energy toward them will fortify that protective filtering.

If it is warmly okay for the constriction inside of you to seemingly ruin everything, especially when it seems that you are so close to finding what you have always yearned for, then that warm okayness is what will allow the constrictive device and the filters inside to fall apart. They need energy to stay together. You can just simply be warmly okay with reaping what you have sown in such a way that it is not a negative to you; it is just simply what it is. You do not have to get rid of or deal with anything. As soon as you are unconditionally okay with the reaping of what you have sown, then that is the sowing of something completely new. And the sowing of that dissolves what you were reaping before.

I see that I'm partially there in some way and I have maybe held onto that, which stopped the flow.

If you were to become awakened, what would allow you to remain awakened would be your permission for any kind of energy at all to come inside you and do anything that it wanted to. If it wanted to take away your awakening, then you would simply remain wide open on the inside. Anything could have your awakening. Anything would be allowed to seemingly ruin it. Anything could interrupt it. Anything could try to put it out.

I hear the truth of what you're saying and I can still feel the resistance in my body.

If you are wide open to being ruined, unconditionally okay within to be ruined in any way inside, then there is nothing that can ruin you. Then, within, you are tenderly invincible. You are untouchable, because it would not matter what were to ruin you, you would be awesomely okay inside. That awesome okayness would be the space and the way of being that you are. There would be nothing that could touch that space then. But if you begin to look around to see if something can take it away, that space is already beginning to shrink and be taken away.

I have a difficulty in my interactions, because on one level I feel very open, and on the other level I fear I'll lose myself in others' agendas.

For you to return to a way of being that is always pure and true, a way of being that requires no discriminating, no judging, no holding together or maintaining, a way of being that is profoundly true in any circumstance at all, then you would be letting everything in as is. If you were to find the Christ or if you were to find the anti-Christ, it would make no difference to your way of being. You would simply, unconditionally, completely and warmly let that energy in: remain in a true way of openness and softness of being, whether what is being encountered is good or evil. You would not be judging. You would simply be giving all of your energy to a way of being that you know is true. Then, if you were to meet the Christ, that would be the only way such a being could access your being, within. Any wanting or needing to get something for yourself would close that access, and nothing real would be able to get in.

If you were to meet a being such as the anti-Christ, and if you were to unconditionally let that energy in, regardless of what that might do to you inside – if you were to completely let it all in and never touch anything to help or preserve or avoid – then there would be nothing that could be reached within you. Deep inside of you, there would be nothing that could be gotten a hold of. That being could reach straight through you and there would be nothing to identify with, nothing to get. Your only protection from meeting an energy like that, is tenderness that has no need of protection at all.

The moment you have any resistance, the moment you do not want to be affected by an energy like that, now it has something to grab. Untrue energy can only grab a holding on inside of you. If there is any measure of holding on – resistance, preference, want of good, or need of pushing away evil – then any kind of untrue energy can have something in you. A little baby is not vulnerable to untrue energy; it is just being itself. Untrue energy goes straight in, can cause inner pain to the baby, but then it goes straight out. It does not get stuck inside. It cannot access the baby's true way of being. It cannot damage reality.

The same is true for untrue energy that you have brought into form, that you have skillfully put in place within to protect yourself or to keep something out. In the same way as the baby does, you can allow that energy to do inside of you anything that it wants; you can allow it to cause pain and seemingly ruin anything. But it will have no place in you. Then, it will have lost its purpose. But as soon as you do not like it, then its purpose remains. And if you really do not like it, that untrue energy will work very hard for its not-okay place in you.

If it is unconditionally and warmly okay for you to lose absolutely all, then that is how much space your being has just gained in you. That is how much room your being now receives to be in you, instead of you. And to that same degree, untrue energy, whether you have put it there yourself or whether it has come from outside of you, will find no place in you to have.

Whatever you lose was never yours, and whatever you could possibly gain will never be for you. In reality there is no room for you. There is only room for your being. That makes it really easy. All of your work is over. And what will happen is your being will take over. It will be where you used to be. The you that you were trying to hold together will all pass away, and the real you will finally live.

It feels like I have a very cunningly constructed web; there are things that are almost the right color but they're not the real thing. But because they're close,

VII. THAT STILL SMALL VOICE

they're difficult to let go of.

They are certainly not worth hanging onto. Awakening is the most wonderful unfolding of a real treasure and even that is not worth hanging onto. We only like our untrue, self-created treasure, because we have a lot of hope invested in it. It has not deeply given us anything, yet we believe that it might, we hope that it will. And it will never really give us anything at all, though it will continue to cost us our energy.

I feel I get so far and then I pull back.

You set up the holding back inside of you a long time ago; now it is finally working for you. So now you get to let it work as well as you have put it together. Now you get to give into your real treasure: your love of openness and softness, in the midst of the holding back pattern you created that tries to undo all of your letting-go. You get to warmly let that pattern be whatever it is, while you simply remain in what you know.

And if that pattern, which you put together, seemingly ruins everything that truth opens up inside of you, then you get to keep on giving into what you know is true. It is your dearest treasure that you can serve truth by simply allowing your way of being to match that of truth itself, that you get to be true, in the midst of all the untrue patterns and constructs that you created for yourself. Then, truth will blossom in any way it is moved to. And if something you yourself created consumes that blossom, that will be warmly none of your business. You are simply residing in the only way you actually know is true – tender, gentle rest within.

I keep going through this process of sifting through these voices and putting them in rank order, trying to work out "is this actually the quietest one?"

Whenever you find what seems to be the quietest one, never assume that there is not a quieter one. The most tender voice within is the only one worth surrendering to.

Until last night, I hadn't really been able to turn off certain things like worries or doubts and they just seemed really loud. Now they don't seem so loud. But the funny thing is that when I got here, when you came into the room today, then things seemed to start to get noisy again.

That is because you have been quieting yourself on the inside. When you walked in, all of those voices came back up in strength, because I am everything that those voices have ever warned you about. They are all voices of rationalization, justification, protection, denial and fear. And you walking into this room will really threaten all of those voices.

While you are away, assuming I don't see you, is there anything else I could be getting on with?

Just let this way of inner openness and softness that you know is true represent your only way of being, at absolutely any personal cost. That's it.

I just thought there was more.

More will happen, but that more right now has no relevance. Right now, the only thing that really does concern you is just a simple way of being that is clear and true: you letting that true way of being completely take over your whole space and have your whole life. That's it. That leaves it really simple. Then, the very, very beginning begins. It is the very, very beginning of your being and the real you being allowed to live this life. And the you that you created for your own wants and needs is finally and simply just out of the way.

The you that you are accustomed to, the one you wanted to be and needed to be, regardless of how loudly it screams, can now from a place

VII. THAT STILL SMALL VOICE

of openness and softness, never be listened to again. You will never argue with it, never believe it, never consult it, even when you are under pressure. You will only be tuned into the quietest voice inside of you. And anything it says you will immediately respond to.

So, it's just looking for that small voice. I don't need to do anything else, like listen to your tapes?

If that still small voice, the tiniest, quietest little voice is drawn to listen to tapes, then that is what you will do. And if that tiny little, quiet, small voice has no preference or need to listen to tapes, then that is not what you will do.

I've been thinking about things that you've said, and I don't know if I should be thinking about them as well as looking for the small voice, or just forget those things.

The smallest voice will speak a language you know on the inside, so you do not have to remember anything I have said on the outside. The outer words represent the smallest voice inside of you. What I am doing, is reacquainting you with that tiniest little voice in you that you have so conveniently covered up, while I am speaking those words. You do not have to remember my words. They will not really help you. But if you remember my way, my way of being, that will open you up. Then you will also remember a lot of words, but what you will love is the way of being you recognize through the words.

What has value is what you taste inside of what I am. There is a flavour to it: a flavour of being, a flavour of the innermost. It is like nourishment and it is like nectar. That is the only part that is worth remembering. When you remember that flavour, then that brings you to exactly the same flavour inside of you, back to a true way of being. That is not instruction, information or teaching as we commonly understand it. A real teacher reacquaints you with a taste that you already know is true, that comes from very, very deep inside of you. That is true teaching.

If anyone ever teaches you – while you are in the midst of an absolutely honest space within, and you are not knowing that innermost flavour, not being quieted and gentled within – then you are listening to a false teacher. Then there will be a whole lot of information that will entertain you and entice you into going inside of your head and playing with information. You will be getting distracted with thoughts and with feelings or excited with something that will supposedly benefit or heal your life, for you. And you will be listening to a false teacher. What you will be hearing is untrue teaching. Believe only what actually touches your being; that will always show you what is true.

When I first came here and saw you, I had some feeling about Jesus and you. I guess it's just because of my upbringing. I'm wondering what your view may be about that. Is it just another story, just moral conscience?

An imaginary Jesus is an imaginary trap. If he is an imaginary Jesus, then the more you need him and want him, the greater you will make him. If he is an imaginary Jesus, and you completely let go of everything in your self-created relationship to that Jesus, then it will all be gone. Nothing will bring it back unless you start giving it energy again.

But if it is a real being of truth who is touching you, then the more awesomely you let go of any mental or emotional attachment, the stronger your knowing of that being will become. Letting-go of all wants and needs and remaining in a true way of inner openness and softness, that is the only way to enlivening a real relationship. That is all. That is the only kind of energy that touches your being in an intimacy of being.

All there is that is really worth believing is just a way that you already know is true, a way of being that connects you to your innermost being and that causes an incredible pull for you to surrender to your innermost at the expense of anything in the outermost. And if that way of being should cause a certain pull in a particular direction, that direction is worth giving into. But in terms of any idea, internal picture, imagination or visualization, they will all take you out of a true way of being. They will all give you something to fixate on and work with in your thoughts and in your feelings. They will keep you busy in your head. What you will continue to experience is an inner ache, instead of the nourishment that only comes from an inner way of being that is tender and true.

If I'm listening to voices in my head and sifting and sorting, my experience is that if they're the noisy ones, there's a lot of energy used up. But when I've been listening and looking for this small voice just recently, I haven't experienced that amount of effort. So I'm assuming, that I'm actually doing that, rather than going through thoughts.

That is true. It is also not the quietest voice in you. The quieter the voice, the more honesty there is in it. There are voices inside of you that are so wonderfully quiet that there is no noise at all. If you were to completely give all of your attention to the very quietest voice in you, it would cost you no energy. And it would give you so much energy. It would cause a flow inside of you that is unstoppable, a kind of flow that heals everything around you and nourishes everything around you and uses up nothing of you. When that kind of flow moves through you, then you become enlivened. There will be the same vitality that you see in tiny little children.

Is the correct approach, when I'm aware that I'm in a thought that's really noisy, just to look somewhere else?

You do not have to look anywhere else. You can keep looking at that loud voice, but from a quietness inside in which you have absolutely no trust in the loud voice at all. You can look at it and to you it will simply be the voice of a fool. The voice will have no meaning to you. It will not even be worth looking away from. If you were to dislike it and look away from it, then it would have something in you; it would have your not liking it.

For you, the looking away from a loud voice will still be worth more than what you have done before. But it gets even finer than that. The freer you become, the less the voices make any difference at all. Then you would not even have a preference. If you actually had a dial inside with which you could turn them off, you would never use the dial. There would be a continual stillness inside that, regardless of any energy moving to disrupt it, would never waver, never change. It would only become quieter yet. There would be room for any kind of energy to move inside of you, go straight to the dial and crank it up. And you would never touch the dial. You would give all your energy just to the stillest, smallest, most tender voice within.

If you are unconditionally okay with any kind of voice inside of you, then you will never do anything with regard to them. Any kind of voice is allowed in. In the warmest way, you just do not listen to them. The only voice that you listen to is that quietest voice. That voice has completely won you. You live in total devotion to that still, small voice. You will never hesitate, never question, never argue, kick or fuss. You will live to give your whole life away to that tiniest little voice inside of you.

The moment the tiny voice moves toward a little bit of a direction, you will go in that direction. And if there is anything in your life that is tied to you that might keep you from moving in that direction, you will cut those ties, just so that you can follow that little voice in the direction it is going. You will live to serve that little voice, and you will never look to that little voice to give you something; you want nothing in return. You live to give all – all the time.

Then your innermost being gets to live in flow – right from the innermost all the way through into every part of the outermost of you as consciousness, right through all of your mental, emotional, physical, intuitional and volitional surface vehicles – and those vehicles of expression will begin to open up like an accordion. They begin to expand, they begin to enlarge, and the flow simply occupies everything that opens up inside of you. There will be mental development that will

VII. THAT STILL SMALL VOICE

not parallel anything you have experienced, emotional depth that will astound you to the core. And anything that begins to blossom in all that opening up will be your dearest treasure to give away to that tiny little voice. You will exist only to give yourself away.

That tiny little voice is just the fineness of being inside of your innermost, flowing just a tiny little bit, very lightly and very tenderly. Let that be you, instead of creating a you for yourself through wants, desires, hopes and dreams. You can give up all your dreams until there is only one deep dream left: the dream that your innermost gets to have anything and everything inside of you; that it gets to have all of the space that you have ever occupied. That is your only real dream.

You will have all sorts of other little dreams in your life, and they will all be wonderfully shallow to you. They will just be play. You can give all of those little dreams to your innermost as well, so that it has something to move up inside of and flow with. Live to offer up everything that is in form for that which is formless in you. Then you will be a real human, from the innermost all the way through to the outermost. And there will be no ego. Consciousness will be free, totally free. It is the only way of being that is actually, really true.

That is your reason and your purpose for being here. You have no other purpose at all. Then any issue that you could ever hold onto could only be a distraction from living for your innermost. Issues are only usurpers of being; they are made-up ways of being to steal space.

Scientists seem to think that the mind itself is inherently complicated and that consciousness is therefore a mysterious thing. I was just wondering what your thoughts on that would be?

In reality, no scientist studying consciousness truly knows what he or she is talking about. A scientist can only perceive. A scientist can only look at something at a distance, study it and draw conclusions. And the conclusions could just as easily be correct as they could be completely out. A scientist cannot really know what kind of conclusion he or she is drawing regarding consciousness, unless that scientist's way of being in consciousness is profoundly true. And then he or she would not merely be studying it, that scientist would be living and realizing consciousness, reality, truth.

My question is whether or not consciousness is mysterious.

How do you define mysterious?

Something which cannot be known or experienced. Something which cannot be quantified; something which cannot be answered.

Nothing in life or the universe is mysterious. Nothing in consciousness is mysterious. But everything to consciousness is wonderfully mysterious. Everything consciousness sees that is a mystery to it causes a pull, and then consciousness moves straight inside of that which is mysterious to it. Once inside, consciousness completely opens itself up, recognizes the reality of it and integrates that. Consciousness merges with the unknown and makes it intimately known to itself.

True consciousness is free to continuously go into the unknown, integrate it and make it profoundly known to itself. It is in a constant state of expansion and integration, and it never ends. As that expansion moves outward into absolutely everything that is presently in form, at exactly the same time, consciousness is going inward, deeper and deeper into what is formless – deeper and deeper and deeper.

Do you think it's possible to define consciousness in any scientific way, or do you think scientists are just wasting their time?

If scientists theorize in defining consciousness, they are not being in the time they are spending theorizing. If someone who is really awakened to consciousness defines consciousness, that person is being in a realization of his or her time. Scientists can only come up with new

VII. THAT STILL SMALL VOICE

information. If they are using the mental vehicle alone to study and define that information, that is of no real value.

A real scientist is any consciousness expanding into the unknown: the unknown of everything that is in form and at the same time, the unknown of everything that is presently formless, and integrating these in the process. That is a real scientist.

Is there a movement of being in me to ask you a question?

There is a movement of being within you that addresses me, and there is a response back in relation to that.

I experience such a strong pull, a movement of being. As I asked myself the question that I just asked you, that pull started to grow a bit, and when you answered me it was really clear. The nectar of being tends to be when we're communicating. That's basically it. My sense is that truth has me, you have me. Yet at the same time there's that voice that also wants to have you, wants to have the nectar.

You can have what I am as a way of being – what I am as a source of that true way of being – just not your way. You can have me only in the way that is congruent with your innermost. In that way, you can have anything that you would want. Anything. There is no limitation, no confinement. You already identify with me that way, and when we are communicating directly, it is easy for you to be in that way that moves your being, only it is quite narrow.

Isn't that ease of communicating with you because you kind of touch me or pull me out, into you?

Yes. But deep within, you already know how to be in that way, because there is a narrow knowing of how to respond. So a flow exists. A relationship or a bond of being exists.

Within that bond, there is the potential for a lot of inner travel; there is a lot more that could happen. But when I am communicating with someone else, your present narrowness of being will have to broaden and expand for you to participate in that same relationship that I would then be flowing in, the same kind of bond of being. Your narrow way of being will have to open up for you to be able to encompass what is happening within me, even when the communication is not presently directed toward you. The more your depth and breadth of being expand, the less our bond of being will be limited and confined by their narrowness. As the expansion of what you are as a being grows, so will your communication, participation and travel with what I am as a being grow.

The only way that your way of being can broaden is by dropping more deeply within. The heart or you as awareness dissolves and becomes so much more wonderfully fine. Then your innermost would have what I am, in depths and breadths of being that you could not even imagine. And that will happen if you keep giving into what you know is true. It is inevitable. If you keep giving you away to this way of being that you love, keep trading your space for that very tender way of being inside to have another place to be in, keep sacrificing you, then it is certain. And you will keep going deeper and deeper and deeper inside of me, inside of my way of being that you know is true.

I keep representing outside of you a depth of what is within you. The more you give into that way of being, the further you will end up inside of what I am, and the deeper your own being will open up inside of you. This really wonderful relationship will be happening – a relationship of being.

That relationship of being is you letting your space be owned and mastered by what you know I am, while I keep letting my space and what I am be owned and mastered by that little part I know in you, that keeps opening up and softening. I let that space in you master everything that I am. I give myself away to you.

So we have this relationship of response. It is a relationship of love,

VII. THAT STILL SMALL VOICE

in truth. There is a flow of in-loveness of being, a flow of intimacy. It is innermost intimacy. And to what you really are as a being, it is irresistible, only because you know that it is true. And the only thing it touches inside of you is your being.

Truth can only find itself in love with truth. Truth is not personal in the way we are accustomed to understanding it, yet it is absolute intimacy of being. It is the only true satisfaction of being that ever was or will be. Truth is not a mystery; its greatest secrets are yours to know through simple honesty and surrender to what that honesty reveals. It is your capacity as consciousness to really live and truly develop as a human being. The moment you taste it, you are irresistibly drawn to be nourished by its goodness, satisfied by its wholeness. Truth is consummate freedom of consciousness. And you will never reach an end.

For more information visit
www.johnderuiter.com

Complimentary Audio Download

To receive your complimentary free audio download, visit
johnderuiter.com/bookaudio and follow the instructions.

USE COUPON CODE:

UNVEILING

google

Hacking trauma with the Wim Hof Method

foundmyfitness.com

Recession profit secrets

1. Wealth is collected — no work
2. Don't let banks burn your $'s
    A. The investments are worth more. —
        loophole
3. Multiply not add to $.